The Jewish Heart
Essays on Jewish Sensitivities

The Jewish Heart

Essays on Jewish Sensitivities

by

RABBI J. SIMCHA COHEN

KTAV PUBLISHING HOUSE, INC.
HOBOKEN, NEW JERSEY

Library of Congress Cataloging in Publication Data

Cohen, J. Simcha.
  The Jewish heart.

  1. Sermons, American—Jewish authors. 2. Jewish
sermons—United States. 3. Festival-day sermons, Jewish.
I. Title.
BM740.2.C55   1985   296.4'2   84-27837
ISBN 0-88125-065-1

MANUFACTURED IN UNITED STATES OF AMERICA

Contents

A Definition

The heart understands: it discerns.
—*Berachot 61a*

The Jewish heart is a finely honed sensitivity to the needs, emotions, and feelings of others. Accordingly, it is an other-directed rather than a self-centered concern.

It is a discipline that forges a symbiotic fusion of heart and mind. It is, therefore, a learned condition, not a natural state.

Character traits are rooted in Torah principles, but all life experiences serve as models for inspiration.

Holidays are not viewed as mere ritual events but as primary symbolic experiental forms to convey moral concerns.

The optimum Jew has a Jewish heart. It is what makes the Jew unique.

Introduction

Torah is more than the collective teachings of the Jewish faith. It is a discipline that molds values and lovingly shapes the contours of character. Accordingly, it permeates all tiers of personal and social concerns. *The Jewish Heart* is an expression of such a value system. Each essay defines a self-contained, independent trait of character. Yet the totality expresses the unique moral essence of the Jew.

Originally, most of the ideas were created for oral expression through the medium of sermons, lectures, and discussions at Congregation Shaarei Tefila, Los Angeles, California. Subsequently, many were published as articles in the Anglo-Jewish media. The ideas spurred an excitement about Jewish values. People began to discuss moral concerns. Community interest in the social character of the Jew became an issue of public dialogue. Is this not what Jewish learning is all about?

Hopefully, *The Jewish Heart* will stimulate a concern for further clarification and study. The highest goal of any Jewish teacher—regardless of the vehicle he utilizes to express his thoughts—is for his students to acquire an enhanced image of Torah and traditional concepts. Accordingly, the goal is to sensitize all to the humanity of Torah itself.

During the summer of 1983, I had a private audience with the Chief Rabbi, HaRav HaGaon R. Avraham Kahana Shapiro, at Heichal Shlomo in Jerusalem. At that time, I presented the Chief Rabbi with a copy of my recently published book, *The 613th Commandment: An Analysis of the Mitzvah to Write a Sefer*

Torah. Noting that the volume was an intense talmudic-halachic discourse, he asked me whether this was my first published book. When I responded in the affirmative, the Chief Rabbi told me the following tale about HaRav HaGaon R. Meir Simcha, the noted talmudic sage and rav of D'vinsk.

R. Meir Simcha, at an early age, wrote two distinct *s'farim* (books). The first was an interpretation of verses in the Pentateuch, entitled *Meshech Hachmah*. The second was a vast commentary on the Rambam's massive halachic opus, entitled *Ohr Samaich*. R. Meir Simcha wished to publish the biblical volume first. He felt that it truly and succinctly expressed his religious philosophy. As such, it should be granted priority of concern. He was advised, however, to alter his plans. Why? He was told that if his first published book would be a biblical analysis, then he would be regarded primarily as a preacher *(darshan)* rather than a talmudic-halachic sage. Accordingly, R. Meir Simcha issued the *Ohr Samaich* first and was lauded as a noted scholar. The same, concluded the Chief Rabbi, may apply to you. It is wise that your first book was a scholarly treatise. Now that you have established your expertise in Talmud with this volume, you may concentrate upon other subject matter.

Though the ordering of the publication of my thoughts was not motivated by such concerns, it is of interest that such did indeed occur. The essays contained in *The Jewish Heart* are truly an integrated expression of my religious value system. They define the optimum Jew.

Throughout the process of creativity, my beloved Rebbitzen Shoshana not only encouraged my efforts but also gently guided my thoughts. She truly manifests an inner, instinctual concern for compassion and Torah values.

To our children Malkah Rachel (née Cohen) and Baruch Shimon Gurvich (and our first grandchild, Esther Leah Rivkah), Matisyahu Nachum, Yehudah Zvi and Deena, a *Birchat Kohan BeAhavah* for the blessing of Torah to infuse their lives.

Special tribute and appreciation must be granted to the mentors of our family, unique parents who serve as models for Torah values and whose wise thoughts are intertwined within the fine fabric of all expressed herein: My father, HaRav HaGaon Rav Meyer Cohen (z.l.), former Executive Director of the Union of Orthodox Rabbis of the United States and Canada, and author of *Helkat Meir*, volumes I and II; my mother, Rebbitzen Itka Cohen; my father-in-law, HaRav HaGaon Rav Yaakov Nayman, the famed Brisker Talmid Chacham and Rav of Congregation Adat B'nai Yisroel, Chicago, Illinois; and my mother-in-law, Rebbitzen Chaya Nayman. It is they who have infused our lives with meaning and joy. It is their love of Torah that has graced our lives and molded our Jewish souls.

I. Jewish Sensitivities and Character

1. Love and Hate

Love is good. Hate is bad. Such is the popular orientation toward these emotional characteristics. Yet it may be demonstrated that love may be a form of hate, for love may manifest a passionate frenzy that is hateful and harmful to others. This concept may be gleaned from the following well-known biblical tale (I Kings 3).

Two women came before King Solomon for judgment. Both had recently given birth to sons. Yet at birth one child died. The problem was that each woman claimed the living child as her own. King Solomon tested the emotional and maternal timber of the women by ruling that the child must be killed and half of it granted to each mother. One woman refused to accept such a cruel decision and cried out her wish that the child be granted to the other rather than be killed. This woman was subsequently proclaimed as the true mother of the child.

What was the motivation of the false mother? What benefit would accrue to her in caring for another's child? Would she not know that the child was not hers?

The Talmud notes that one who has no child is comparable to a dead person (*Nedarim* 64b). This suggests that there is an instinctual drive to do good for another. Though one may actualize this inner love by caring for strangers, its total emotional fulfillment is accomplished through the process of parenthood. Coupled to this is the recognition that not everyone will accept love from another. Being the recipient of love entails debts of gratitude. Some are averse to the obligation crystallized by such love. In a parent-child relationship it is natural to both give and receive love. The process permits intense rela-

3

tionships. Accordingly, the lack of children withholds from the parent the social aspect of giving parental love. This is comparable to death.

This love may be so passionate that it may even be extended to a strange child. Not knowing the real mother, the child would assume that the woman caring for him and loving him was his own mother. Thus the false mother could simulate the natural loving relationship of a mother and a son.

Yet what about the real mother? What about her feelings of hurt and loss? How could the false mother extend love when each kind gesture was a lie? Each act of love a theft from the real mother? Was not such love cruel? Was not the false mother hateful to the real mother? How could she give so much love to her child when she was simultaneously so full of hate?

From this story we learn that love can be a form of hate. In fact, both emotions can coexist. A person can love so intensely as not to perceive the hate or harm caused to another. One may be blinded by the passions of love to see only the good. One does not perceive the harm or hate that results (even to oneself).

So love is not always a virtue. It may mask corrosive, offensive attitudes. The difficulty is that intense love is such an emotional state that it is oblivious to reason and logic. What's worse is that people in love assume that all probing, pragmatic questions emanate from those who simply do not understand the blissful state of loving emotions.

King Solomon, therefore, ruled that the child should be killed and each claimant mother should be granted one-half. The king astutely believed that "true love" would not tolerate harm. The real mother would manifest self-sacrifice rather than destruction. That is the test of love: the ability to seek out the benefit of another rather than only personal pleasure. (See R. Chayyim Schmuelevitz, *Sichot Mussar*, 5733.

Who has the will or wisdom to test the components of love? Who, better yet, wishes to submit his or her love to a test?

2. To Love Means to Say I'm Sorry

Yesterday my feelings were hurt. You embarrassed me. You insulted me. You verbally mutilated my pride. I felt so ashamed that I could not contain myself. Yet today you apologized. You said you were sorry. You told me of your remorse. You regretted all that you said and did to inflict pain upon me. You wanted me to forgive you so that we should be friends again.

But how can I ever forget yesterday's pain? Does today's apology erase the torment of yesterday? Is not the phrase "I'm sorry," therefore a meaningless gesture?

Yet Jewish law mandates that upon the expression of an apology I must tolerantly forgive all wrongs. Why? What role does an apology play in cementing meaningful human relationships?

Scripture defines social activity as being garbed by an aura of love. As it is written, "And thou shall love thy neighbor as thyself" (Leviticus 19:18). Rav Yitzchok Hutner, a master teacher of mine, noted that true love manifests two distinct qualities, for one is simultaneously both a "lover" and a "beloved." A lover is one who actively crystallizes love to another. He cares and shows concern for another's needs. As a result, he, in return, becomes an object of love, a person who is the recipient of his beloved's active fellowship and love.

An insult jars the relationship. It presents the injured party with an excuse for not returning love. How can I or why should I make you an object of my love, when you acted in such a nonloving, hurtful manner? You are not deserving of my love. By insulting me you demonstrated that I am not your beloved—so why should you be mine?

Your apology does not erase the hurt. I remember it well. It still is painful. But you've expressed an interest in reviving our relationship. You want me to be once again the object of your love. You've apologized. You wish to shower me with friendship. You've made the initial move to renew our relationship. You've taken away from me the "excuse" for not being kind to you. You love me. How can I not reciprocate by making you the object of my love once again? So the phrase "I'm sorry" is not an empty gesture. No, not at all. It is the reaffirmation of love itself.

3. Innocent Victims of Anger

Why is that person angry with me? Why did he scream at me? I never harmed him. I never did anything to denigrate his character. I'm positive that even unwittingly I have never even caused him any adverse reaction. I'm innocent of all blame. So, why is he so hateful to me? Three theories are suggested.

• This person woke up today in an angry mood. Some problem is bothering him. I'm merely the first person he met to vent his spleen. It is a pure accident that I happened to encounter him before he had an opportunity to rid himself of his anger on somebody else. Such are the quirks of fate. By being the recipient of such negative behavior I may even be serving a beneficial function to society. Others, now, may peacefully meet this man and engage in a meaningful dialogue and relationship. It's possible that he needed such a therapeutic ventilation of emotion. As a result, my remorse over being victimized is somewhat salvaged by the realization of the healing process that I crystallized.

• I may deserve a divine punishment for some sin I committed. Instead of a great affliction God was good to me. He made me the innocent victim of hate. All I suffered was a ruffling of my ego and a few bad emotional moments. Thank God it was not worse.

• I may have performed a favor in behalf of this person. A tale will clarify this issue.

Two men were standing in line to purchase tickets at the railroad station of a large city. The second person overheard the conversation between the first man and the ticket agent. "Listen, I'm a wealthy man. I must be on this train to enable me to get home before my Shabbat. I don't know what happened to me, but I simply do not have any more cash. Please, I'm only two pennies short of the price of the ticket. I'll send you the money next week. Please, give me the ticket." "Ah," said the second person. "I know you. You're Reb Hershel, the great philanthropist of our little town. Don't worry at all. Don't even argue. Here, I'll loan you two pennies for your ticket."

By coincidence both were seated next to each other on the train. The wealthy man gazed with astonishment as the other person took out a diary and wrote, "On Friday, Erev Shabbat, I, Zalman the shoemaker, loaned two pennies to Reb Hershel the philanthropist." "What are you doing?" sputtered Reb Hershel. "I borrowed two little pennies from you and you're making such a Megillah out of it. Is it necessary to record for perpetuity such a measly transaction in your diary? Big deal! Two pennies!" "Oh, no, Reb Hershel, it is a big deal. Two pennies may not be a lot of money. Yet if not for this sum you would not be able to be home for Shabbat. My feeling is that sooner or later you are going to hate me for knowing of your problem. It goes against your grain that you, the great, affluent leader, had to come on to me, a nobody, for a favor. As a result, instead of rewarding me, you'll punish me. So I'm recording that the favor was worth only two pennies. Accordingly, when you attempt to punish me, just a reminder, no more than the value of two pennies should you extract from my hide."

How true! Some people just cannot live with gratitude. They hate those whom they owe the most. The sense of obligation generates a dependency that their character cannot tolerate. They don't want to owe anything to anybody. These ingrates corrode the good patterns that cement society together.

For this reason Judaism defines kind behavior as *gomlai chasadim* (the repayment of kindness). All life, all that we have, is but a debt that we owe others. There is no such thing as meaningful life without gratitude.

So, being an innocent victim of hate is not necessarily a dysfunctional experience. I may have been selected to experience hate as a means of healing the sick or to make me appreciate that my past merits mitigated a divine punishment. I also have been given a moral test of character, an opportunity to personally view the degradation of ingratitude. But this should not negatively impact on my behavior. I like people and recognize my debt to others. I want people to be nice to me. The hateful ingrate is a loner. No one will help him again. But that's his problem—not mine.

4. Jewish Moral
Overtones of Silence

Silence is generally acclaimed as a moral virtue. Indeed, the popular idiom is that "silence is golden." The Talmud parallels such a sentiment by the statement, "A word is worth a *sela*, and silence, two" (*Megillah* 18a). Thus, silence is granted a greater moral valuation than speech.

Yet no action or inaction has a universal claim to virtue. Love is not always commended, nor anger condemned. Are there not times when joy is inappropriate and compassion an error? Human emotions are morally neutral without consideration of specific situational conditions. This suggests that silence must manifest a negative as well as a positive moral evaluation. Thus, it is necessary to analyze the social and religious component of silence in order to assess its moral overtones.

A popular rabbinic saying is that *syag l'chachma sh'teeka*—"silence is the gate of wisdom." Thus, silence is not categorized as wisdom but, rather, as a vehicle to safeguard wisdom. Its role is to facilitate the acquisition of knowledge. A person who is able to listen to another has the capacity of digesting information. A person who cannot be verbally still is one so wrapped up in his own importance that the views of others cannot be appreciated or even learned. Such a person exudes the image that others have nothing to teach him. Such a person cannot acquire wisdom; for wisdom is a constant process of learning new information. The nonsilent is also a static personality. What he was is what he is now and what he shall be; for he never has the patience to learn from others. He is too busy talking to learn.

In addition, such a person cannot truly experience the fine qualities of compassion, love, and justice. Without hearing the plight of another, it is virtually impossible to truly understand the needs of anyone. Empathy requires the role of silence for emotional comprehension. As a result, silence is the gate that sustains sensitivity and generates knowledge.

Another positive aspect of silence is that it is garbed with the mantle of trust. As Proverbs notes, *V'neh'eman ruach m'chaseh davar,*—"A trustworthy spirit can conceal a matter" (11:13). He who can be silent deserves trust. One reveals the innermost secret of one's heart only to someone who can maintain silence. No one tells private matters to those who cannot sustain verbal discretion. Whether business or social affairs, a promise or assumption of silence is necessary for the exchange of crucial personal ideas or sentiments. Trust opens up secrets. Trust demands a reputation for silence.

It is no wonder that Proverbs notes, "Even a fool when he keeps silent may be thought wise; he who locks his lips is intelligent" (17:28). Yet at times it is wrong to be thought wise, when in fact such a quality is lacking. In a school or in a learning situation it is harmful to assume the guise of wisdom when one is ignorant. *Pirke Avot* contends *"lo ha baishon lamaid* (2:6). A bashful person cannot truly acquire knowledge; for he is embarrassed to publicly note his ignorance. He would rather be silent than tell a teacher of his lack of comprehension. Asking questions and admitting ignorance is essential to the process of learning. The totally silent person is deemed wise but in reality is destroying his intellectual potential. He is corroding the learning process so that his public image may be proper. Thus, the person who values silence to the extent that he withholds speech has no substantive content. Such a person degrades the basic role of human communication.

Silence, moreover, may also be deemed a sin. The Talmud states, "How do we know that a disciple sitting before his master, who sees that the poor man is right and the wealthy man wrong, should not remain silent? Because it is said, *Midvar shekar teerchak*—From a false matter keep far" (*Shevuot* 31a). This case teaches us that silence is a form of falsehood. In other words, it is morally incumbent to speak out and rectify an erroneous legal decision. Even though the case is being judged by the master and not the disciple, and normally it would be considered audacious to contradict one's teacher, still the biblical injunction obligates one to reveal truth. Silence in such a situation is a form of agreement and assent to the error. The silent person, by his inaction, gives the impression that he too agrees with the decision. He becomes an accomplice to the error. Silence, therefore, may sometimes be viewed as moral sanction to immoral activities. It thus assumes the character of cowardice rather than moral value.

Indeed, silence may also reflect a severe defect in the moral timber of a person.

The Talmud states (*Soteh* 11a) that prior to the enactment of the evil decrees which enslaved the Jews in Egypt, Pharaoh sought the counsel of three sages. Job was silent at this meeting and subsequently was punished by the Almighty for his silence by the affliction of pain. Yet punishment in the Bible generally relates in some form to the nature of the crime. In this situation the punishment of pain in no way relates to the sin of Job. Also, it is necessary to determine the nature of Job's immoral behavior. What sin did he commit by being silent? Yes, his silence may be construed as a form of acquiescence to the slavery of the Jews promulgated by Pharaoh. But is it not possible that Job firmly believed that any action or statement on his part would be to no avail? What impact would his demurral have upon Pharaoh? How could one individual go against the mighty legions and the powerful Egyptian military machine? Sensing, therefore, the futility of any contrary position, Job merely was silent. Was this silence such a grievous crime that Job was subsequently punished by the agony of constant physical pain and sickness?

The punishment of pain was a divine lesson to Job, and through him to all mankind, that the argument of futility is not morally adequate to sustain silence in times of danger. Job was afflicted with such severe ailments that he cried out constantly because of the unbearable agony of the pain. Why did he cry? Why did he publicly bemoan his physical pain? Did he not know that screaming and moaning do not help the condition? Is it not futile to moan when one is in pain? The answer is that it is the nature of man to cry out when he hurts. Crying does not stop the pain but, rather, gives evidence that the pain exists. It is the verbal manifestation that something internally is wrong. The silent person is basically the one who does not poignantly feel pain. All is well—there is no reason to cry. Job's reaction to his own plight, and his silence in the face of impending danger to Jews, proved that Job felt no internal pain when Jews were killed. Job cried over his personal problems, not over pogroms to Jews. The enslavement and the possible ultimate destruction of the Jewish people did not disturb Job's emotional tranquility. Had Job been a friend to the Jewish people, then the silence would have been impossible. The natural human strands of emotions would have evoked a verbal crescendo of pain. Silence was, therefore, evidence of no concern and no personal involvement. For this reason, Job's silence was marked as a message of immorality. So, too, in the modern world, American Jewry will be judged not only for what we say and do, but also by the impact of our silence in the face of danger to our people. Each Jew must feel the pain of another—each Jew should cry out when another Jew is hurt. Silence means we simply do not care.

Thus, silence is neither good nor bad, right nor wrong. It all depends on the situation. Maybe this is the true meaning of "silence is the gate of wisdom." A person's silence—that is, when he speaks out, when he cries, when he withholds his speech—that is the true sign of wisdom.

5. Honor to Friends: Each Person Unique

Tradition has it that R. Akiva's students mysteriously died in one year during the time span between Pesach and Shavuot. The Talmud contends that their death was a divine punishment for the failure of the students to manifest *kavod* (honor) to each other (*Yevamot* 62b).

Such a rationale is difficult to comprehend; for those who died were neither illiterate nor immoral. They were students of Torah, disciples of the pious, gentle sage R. Akiva. How was it possible that such scholars were bereft of common decency and neglectful of moral concerns?

It is suggested that each student considered himself the equal of his peers. There was a bond of unity amongst them. Just as it is foolish to grant *kavod* to one limb over another, so too did the students believe that the extension of *kavod* to friends and peers was an unimportant gesture. One doesn't give *kavod* to peers—one grants love and friendship.

Indeed, are not the garbs of sophistication and the social veneer of dignified behavior discarded in the company of friends? Is not a meeting of peers the proper setting to just be "oneself"—one's real self—without the mask of social obligations? *Kavod* is reserved for rabbis, teachers, parents, senior citizens—but not for friends. Should not peers be considered equals?

How many people come home at night and change their attire to be informal and relaxed. They seek an aura of equality

14

far removed from the stuffiness of dignity and the structure of formal relations. Yet the Talmud contends that such social patterns have overtones of immoral action. Why? For such behavior is inimical to the nature of Torah scholars.

Kavod is the deference granted to a person in recognition that he possesses a unique, elevated status. A scholar is honored for the knowledge he has acquired. A communal leader is granted *kavod* for the service he has provided. Each person is unique. Each person has a quality better than his peer. No two people are equal in attributes. No teacher has value if all students are considered equal. Each child has a trait which must be enhanced. Each scholar has a quality lacking in another. Jewish ethics is based upon the reality of distinctions. Some things are good; others are bad. Some traits are to be acquired; others should be avoided at all costs.

Jewish scholars cannot treat other scholars as equals. Each is a person from whom one may learn. Each is a friend and yet also a teacher. The error of R. Akiva's disciples was that they erroneously believed that Torah may only be acquired from master teachers—not from friends. This is a flaw in Jewish ethics.

The moral is that every man is both student and teacher. That social life is the true seminar of values.

Who is closer to a person than his mate? Is not a man's wife also his best friend? Yet the Talmud notes that "a man must love his wife like [he loves] himself, yet honor her more than himself" (*Yevamot* 62b). The honor to a mate is the firm recognition that each is respected for the unique traits that the other does not possess. Each again is simultaneously a teacher and a disciple.

In other words, no peer is my equal—and I am not the equal of anyone. We are different, and we respect that difference.

Another interpretation may be as follows.

Scripture mandates two forms of deference to a parent. A child must honor his parents (*keebud*—Exodus 20:12) and also extend reverence (*morah*—Leviticus 19:3). The Talmud delineates the distinction by stating, "What is *morah* and what is *keebud*? *Morah* means that he [or she] must not stand in his father's place nor sit in his place, not contradict his words. . . . *Keebud* means that he must give him food and drink, clothe and cover him" (*Kiddushin* 31b).

What is surprising is that this definition of honor is somewhat different from the generally understood social meaning of the term. In general, to honor someone suggests that one relates to the honoree in a respectful, deferential pattern. The honoree is acclaimed, extolled, and made to feel special and important. Yet the Talmud appears to discount this approach. Instead it notes that verbal expressions of honor are meaningless unless coupled with pragmatic acts of service benefiting a parent. What merit is there to words of deference if acts of service are lacking? Erich Fromm once noted that anyone who says he loves flowers and then fails to water them testifies that his expression of love is meaningless. So too with honor—to honor someone means that one has a finely honed conditioned response of service to the honoree's needs. This was the tragic flaw of R. Akiva's students. They did not believe it necessary to extend themselves to their peers. They believed that parents and teachers must be provided with service but not friends. Considering each counterpart student as an equal, the need of service to such a person was deemed a violation of the sense of equality. They would relate to each other with respect—but beyond words there were no pragmatic acts of service.

This too is the meaning of the talmudic dictum mandating a husband to honor his wife (op. cit.). It is not enough to express words of love to a mate.

It is essential, rather, to ground the verbal platitudes with positive actions. Honor in marriage is the reciprocal response of practical actions which benefit each other.

This tragic flaw (of the students) had to be uprooted; for should it prevail, then the moral contour of future generations would be altered. Children would grow up without a true understanding of *kavod* and its relationship to Torah, to learning, and to giving. Each generation has an obligation to preserve the purity of the *Mesora*. This is the role of each scholar, each parent, and each man and woman prior to marriage.

6. The Jewish Social Character

Sociologists maintain that national and ethnic groups possess something called a "social character." This means that there is a certain pattern of behavior which sets a group distinctly apart from others and is essential to an understanding of their life existence.

What then is the social character of the Jewish people? What behavioral pattern marks the Jew? the Talmud (*Yevamot* 79a) suggests a unique formulation of the Jewish social identity. It says, *Gimel seemanim b'ooma zoo: rachmoniim, baishonim, v'gomlay chasadim*—the Jewish nation has three innate qualities:

1. *Rachmoniim*—they are compassionate.
2. *Baishonim*—they manifest shame.
3. *V'gomlay chasadim*—they are kind and considerate.

Since these three qualities identify the essential nature of the Jewish people, it is necessary to define each characteristic as well as to note their mutual interrelationships; for it is apparent that all three characteristics relate to each other.

Rachmoniim: Compassionate

A compassionate person poignantly feels the sorrows of others. At the sight of the poor, the sick, the weak, the lonely, a feeling of unease is developed.

A compassionate person does not like to perceive misfortune. Problems generate a Pavlovian response of aid. The problem must be resolved in order for the compassionate person to feel once again at ease. The disturbance of the equilibrium must be eliminated. This is the first characteristic.

18

Gomlay Chasadim—Kindness

Kindness is qualitatively different from compassion. A compassionate person reacts to outward stimuli. A problem exists. A person is in trouble. The compassionate person responds to the external problem. Once the problem is eliminated, the compassionate person is once again at ease with himself. Life may be enjoyed to its fullest dimension as long as the *rachaman*—the compassionate person—is unaware or not involved with *tzoris*.

A *baal chesed*—a kind person—has an inner need to help others. He is motivated by internal stimuli. He is not happy unless he can share that happiness with others. A kind person extends himself both to the rich and the poor. Do not affluent people need kindness? Is not a fine word, a gracious gesture, a cordial smile an act of glorious kindness? Abraham was the highest example of kindness. He went to search for guests. Even while ill, he wanted to bestow his gracious hospitality upon others.

Kindness—*chesed*—does not await problems before it is bestowed upon others. It is a self-motivating force that is eased by the constant expression of sharing with others.

Indeed, kindness is described by the Talmud as *gomlay chasadim—gomlay*, i.e., the repaying of kindness. The kind person recognizes that all that he has and possesses is a result of a kindness granted to him by someone else. His stature, his wealth, his abundance, his joy are all due to somebody's previous generous nature. All he does is repay that kindness by expressing *chesed* to others. He seeks recipients; he looks for customers. His happiness is complete only when others are happy too.

Boosha—Shame

The true meaning of this term is awe and modesty. It is the quality of humbleness which is manifested by one who recognizes greatness. It is found only in those who have an appreciation of stature. One stands apart from a great person and is modest or ashamed to intrude upon him. A person without values has no respect for others. A person without values cannot be embarrassed. It is an inner recognition that others have merit and value. *Boosha* is, therefore, a fine fabric of awe, respect, and modesty to values, people, and institutions. It is the necessary criterium for *yirat shamayiim*—religious piety. This means that even when the Jew is involved in expressions of compassion and kindness he is modest and humble. His good deeds are not patronizing or disrespectful. He is, rather, ashamed that he cannot do even more. This is the second characteristic of the Jewish personality.

It is interesting to note that the scriptural verse cited by the Talmud to substantiate kindness being a basic ingredient of the Jewish personality is Genesis 18:19, wherein God states, "I know Abraham, for he will command his children and household after him, that they may keep the way of the Lord, to do righteousness and justice." And yet nowhere does this verse overtly speak of kindness. All it relates is that Abraham will teach his children justice and righteousness. *Tzedakah* is not necessarily kindness. The *chesed*—the kindness—is the fact that Abraham will ensure that his children will do good deeds. That is *chesed*. That is what Abraham did. He guaranteed that his children would follow in his path. The term *kee y'dativ*—"I know him"—is translated by Rashi to mean, "I love him." For knowledge and love mutually reinforce each other. The more knowledge that one has about another, states Rashi, the more one loves him. The more one is loved, the more knowledge is sought. Abraham is loved because he shares his personality traits with his children; his children also will love kindness.

This is the Jewish social character.

This is what Judaism is all about.

7. Definition of a Friend
(A Modern Adaptation of an Ancient Tale)

"My son, I've called you to be with me; for in my last moments of life I have something to give you. It's not money. Yet it's more important, for it's the one principle that will give meaning to life itself. Get a friend."

"What? Is this what you want me to have from you? Money, cash, land, jewels you don't provide to me. But, rather, something more valuable. A lesson for life itself. But I already have friends. Numerous friends. Is this the message you've learned from your life? Is this bequest profound? No, Dad, I see it as a simple, commonplace concept. Please excuse me, but I'm shocked that you feel that I would value such a bequest."

"My son, you have friends?"

"Yes—and I'm ashamed to tell anyone of your great inheritance to me."

"Let's test the quality of your friends. Please, my son, heed me. Go and slaughter the young goat in the backyard. Don't cleanse yourself from the blood. But simply place the remains in a large sack. Go to your friends. Knock on their doors. Let them see the blood on your hands as well as the blood oozing from the sack. Ask them for a favor. Tell them you wish to bury the contents of your sack in their backyard. Tell them that you cannot explain to them the motivation for your request nor can you describe the contents of the sack. It's a favor you seek. You wish permission to bury the sack without any explanation at all. You seek their compliance as a gesture of friendship."

21

The young man did as his father bade him to do. Looking disheveled, bloody, and quite suspicious, he began the process of requesting help from his friends.

"Yes, who is it?"

"It's me, your friend Shimon."

"What can I do for you, Shimon?"

"I need a favor. A big one. Please ask no questions as to why, but may I have permission to bury my sack in your yard?"

"What? Shimon, you look peculiar. There's blood all over your hands and your face. Tell me what's going on?"

"I said no questions. Believe me I know what I'm doing. We've been friends for many years. Just let me go in the back and bury this sack."

"No way! Shimon, you have chutzpah coming here in the middle of the night with such a request. Something strange and maybe illegal seems to have occurred. Either you tell me all the details or simply forget it altogether."

"I said I can't explain. Will you give me permission to bury my sack?"

"No, and please don't bother me again."

Shimon found the door closed in his face. As he went to all his other so-called friends a similar response took place. No one helped him. Word of his bizarre appearance and request spread throughout the neigborhood. As he approached certain homes the doors wouldn't even be opened for him to make his statement. He became like a leper whose presence made others flee for fear of social contact or contagion.

"Well," said the old man, "did your friends help you?"

"No, not at all. Some wouldn't even speak with me. In fact, after tonight, I doubt whether they'll ever speak with me again."

"Shimon, my son, please go to my half-friend Chayyim. Tell him that you're Yaakov's son. Ask him to bury your sack in his backyard."

In the early hours of the morning, Shimon knocked on the door of his father's half-friend Chayyim.

"Hello, who's there?"

"It's me, Shimon, the son of Yaakov. I need a favor. My father said that you would help me. Please, may I bury this sack in your yard now?"

"Certainly. Come with me. I'll help you."

Without any question whatsoever, Chayyim helped the young man bury the sack. Subsequently, he gave him the opportunity to wash himself and his clothes. His only remark was a request for regards to be sent to the old father, Yaakov.

The son returned to his father full of wonder and amazement.

"Now that's a friend," he said. "This old man did more for me than all of my friends together. But why did you call him your half-friend? That was a real act of friendship."

"No, my son," said the father. "Chayyim is only a half-friend. He's not a true whole friend. A whole friend does more than Chayyim is able to do. Allow me to explain by means of a tale.

"Once there were two friends. One lived in Jerusalem, the other in Alexandria. On a day when the friend from Jerusalem visited Alexandria a robbery took place. Since he was a stranger the sultan's men captured the friend from Jerusalem, accused him of the crime, and placed him in the town square prior to his public execution. As the friend from Alexandria saw his old friend from Jerusalem being prepared to be killed, he called out to the sultan.

" 'Release this man. He is innocent. I am the guilty party. I am the thief. Kill me, not him.'

"When the Jerusalem friend heard this, he in return called out: 'No, that man is not guilty. I retract my former statements of innocence. I really was the thief. Kill me, not the other man. Please, I really am guilty.'

"The sultan, upon hearing both men demanding death for themselves, each willing to die so that his friend might live, knew instinctively that both could not be guilty of the crime. An investigation was launched and the true culprit was apprehended."

The old man concluded. "A whole friend is willing to give up even life itself for his friend. A half-friend will sacrifice all monetary possessions—everything except life itself. My son, find a friend."

Now, how many friends do we have?

8. The Test of Humility

Humility is a positive religious value essential to moral character. Indeed, no true "mentsh" is arrogant. Abraham, the father of the Jewish religion, even set an example of humbleness. In his prayers for the salvation of the people of Sodom, Abraham depreciated his merits by contending that he was but "dust and ashes" (Genesis 18:27). The Dubno Maggid clarified the phrase as follows: "Dust, dirt, sand may be crystallized and formed into objects of value. They have a potential future use even if they have no past. Ash, however, has a past. It once was something. It had a form and a value. Yet it has no future usage. Abraham, therefore, maintained his total humility before God. He was 'dust and ashes.' He lacked any past accomplishments [like dust] and perceived no grandeur for the future [like ash]."

The humble man of today, however, may not be assessed by the expression of such thoughts. Indeed, such a person may be overshadowing a contemptuous arrogant personality. An example:

It is told that Rabbi Yonathan Eibshitz noted a great philanthropist and leader of the community praying with intense fervor. This man prostrated himself before the holy ark and cried, "O God, I am dust and ash. I am nothing. I came from nothing. Please, have mercy upon me." Subsequently, the same person was noted scolding an official trustee of the synagogue for not granting him the honor of being called to the Torah. "Don't you know who I am," the philanthropist raged.

"Why I deserve an honor more than anyone else in this synagogue." Rav Yonathan was shocked at such words. He approached the philanthropist and asked, "How could you express such sentiments? Are you not the same person who cried out, 'I am nothing'?"

"Ah," said the man. "Rabbi, you don't understand. When I talk with God, I recognize that I'm nothing compared to Him. But when I relate to people, especially a man like this synagogue trustee, then it's a completely different matter. Such a person should have respect for my position and status."

In other words, humbleness before God is not enough. True humbleness requires humility before man.

9. Misplaced Humility

"To every thing there is a season, and a time to every purpose under heaven: . . . A time to weep, and a time to laugh"
(Ecclesiastes 3:1–4).

How true: special situations guide our expressions of emotion and mold their contours. Woe to the person who laughs at a funeral or bewails the joy of a wedding. Accordingly, the constant manifestation of but one single emotion for diverse experiences is a serious flaw of character. Such a person is indifferent to reality. He is living in a world of his own mind.

So, too, with moral traits. They must be rooted in reality.

In general, for example, humility and modesty are lauded as commendable virtues. Yet there are specific periods of time when modesty represents a moral flaw, a weakness of character, and an abrogation of responsibility.

The prophet Samuel reproaches King Saul for his disobedience by saying: "Though thou be little in thine own sight, art thou not head of the tribes of Israel? . . . wherefore then did thou not hearken to the voice of the Lord?" (I Samuel 15:17, 19—JPS). The implication is that the motivation for Saul's disobedience was his humility and trait of self-depreciation. The king even admits to this characterization by stating, "I feared the people and hearkened to their voice" (ibid 15:24).

Samuel, the prophet, was concerned that Saul should behave like a king. A king should lead and not be led. The position of leadership demands action, not self-doubt and

27

humility. The people must follow the direction of the king. A leader is more than the mouthpiece of the masses. He should be decisive, he should coalesce action. He should initiate thought. He must guide. A leader who doubts his ability, who lacks initiative, who considers his view secondary to all others—such a person is a disservice as a king. Such a person cannot function properly as a leader.

Thus, humility may at times be a misplaced virtue.

The prophet's charge is not only to King Saul but to the leaders of all generations. Indeed, a comparable sentiment is to be noted in our daily prayers. "Return our judges as at first so that they may counsel us . . . and remove from us sorrow and suffering." At first glance a request for judges and a prayer for the removal of anguish appear as two unrelated issues. Yet the fact that they are both combined within one blessing suggests even a cause-and-effect relationship.

People want decisions. They wish certitude for actions. Lack of leaders to make such determinations crystallizes the "sorrow and suffering" of doubt. The prayer, therefore, is not for leaders who are too humble to take action, nor for judges who are too modest to make decisions. Such people should not assume such roles. We pray, rather, for leaders who can lead and judges who are not afraid to judge. It is they who can effectively discharge the aura of doubt and the pain of indecision. That is the role of leaders.

10. Tensions of a Commanded Jew

Who is better? Who should receive a greater reward? The volunteer? Or the person who fulfills his obligations? Simple logic suggests that the volunteer should be rated higher than one who merely meets the requirements demanded of him. For the volunteer has the option of inaction. Indeed, a wide gamut of personal concerns were available to him. He did not have to volunteer his services. The fact that he did shows sincerity, meaning, and affection.

Yet the Talmud contends that Judaism is based upon just the opposite position. R. Hanina rules that "he who is commanded and fulfills such command is greater than he who fulfills it though not commanded" (*Kiddushin* 31a). Tosaphot (ibid.) note that those commanded are granted a greater reward, for under the duress of a command there is tension to violate it.

The meaningful impact of this may be noted in the following tale (I Kings 2).

King David, upon his deathbed, formally instructed his son Solomon to utilize wisdom to destroy his enemy Shimei ben Gera. Upon assumption of his reign, King Solomon made the following declaration to Shimei ben Gera: "You are an enemy of my father, King David, yet he swore not to harm you. Build a house in Jerusalem. As long as you reside in that city you may live. The moment, however, you depart from its borders, you will be killed." Sometime later some of Shimei ben Gera's sheep grazed in an area outside the limits of Jerusalem. Shimei ben Gera went to fetch them, was captured, and was subsequently killed as per the dictate of the king.

Rav Chayyim Shmuelevitz, former dean of the Mirrer Yeshivah in Jerusalem, made the following observations:

• What was the punishment mandating residence in Jerusalem? Some people would consider that a reward rather than a punishment.

• How did King Solomon know that Shimei ben Gera would eventually leave the city?

• Why did Shimei venture out of Jerusalem's boundaries knowing full well that it was a personal capital crime?

King Solomon was aware of a fundamental axiom of human life: that coercion creates rebellion. A person forced to reside in a palace will ultimately view it as a prison. When one is required to do something, the act itself loses its intrinsic luster. It becomes burdensome and onerous. King Solomon knew that sooner or later the urge to rebel—to be independent—would overcome all protective constraints of caution. It was but a matter of time—but Shimei would leave Jerusalem.

So too with commandments. Sooner or later the bondage of commitment corrodes observance. The daily requirement to act and to observe specific rituals becomes oppressive. Man wants to be free, to do that which he and he alone decides is of personal importance. The yoke of the command nettles the free spirit of human character. There is an irresistible, magnetic human drive to cast off all obligations and simply be oneself.

R. Hanina, therefore, says, "He who is commanded and fulfills such command is greater than he who fulfills it though not commanded." The person who not just occasionally but constantly achieves personal joy and meaning by meeting all obligations, such a person is a true "believer." Such action is the test of character. For such a person has sublimated his goals and cares not only for personal pleasure. He is a man of commitment. He is a commanded Jew. He is a person of strength, for he overcame the temptation to seek freedom from obligation.

11. Grab Bagels

Hypocrisy is to be shunned. No one likes a hypocrite, and certainly no one wishes to be so labeled. It is of interest that the desire to be innocent of any aspersions of hypocrisy is utilized as a major excuse for the nonobservance of Jewish traditions.

When Jews who have strayed somewhat from the religious path are asked to observe a specific ritual, the rationale they offer not only for their nonobservance but also to cut short any further inquiries usually goes as follows:

• How can I maintain a kosher home when I do not discriminate outside the home?

• Why pray in your synagogue on Shabbat when I do not observe the Shabbat at all?

• Why observe the traditional laws of mourning when I do not follow any other precepts?

Accordingly, any request for increased observance is countered by an admission of nonobservance in another area. The response generally includes the statement, "I am not a hypocrite." What irks is the final charge. "Rabbi, are *you* asking me to be a hypocrite?"

Such encounters can definitely faze a rabbi. Some rabbis, as a result, have simply given up and preach only to the committed.

What is unique is that intellectual honesty and purity are generally demanded only of religion. Only in the sphere of Jewish ritual observance is hypocrisy to be so denigrated that it is classified as a (legitimate) defense against partial commitment.

People never claim that since they do not always tell the truth, therefore, they must always tell lies. No one contends that since they cheat occasionally, all honesty is to be scorned. Lack of ability to ascend all rungs of religious life does not mean that partial ascent is to be castigated. The higher the goal, the more difficult it is to achieve. In fact, true religious passion and spiritual fervor require years of training. One does not become a religious, spiritual Jew overnight. One cannot succeed in religion by attempting to accomplish all in one period of time. Certain items, however, do require a plunge. Kashrut, for example, does necessitate commitment; for one cannot become kosher dish by dish. Yet inability to do all does not negate the value of what is or has been accomplished. The human personality is not perfect, and it is normal for people to assume obligations and express thoughts that are not part of a total, holistic approach. That is not hypocritical—that is the real world.

The following tale of the Chafetz Chaim suggests a pragmatic approach to the problem.

An old woman who made a living selling bagels had an accident. Some youngsters jostled her basket of wares, and all her bagels fell to the ground. Numerous children pounced upon the strewn bagels, grabbing as much as they could carry, and then ran away. The old woman, sitting on the street, began to cry and bemoan her plight. "Foolish woman," called out a man to her. "If you sit and cry, you'll end up with nothing. *Chap* (grab) some bagels too."

How true. How realistic is this approach. Should Jews merely bemoan their inability to observe all the mitzvot, then they will end up like the old woman with nothing. Grab bagels! A *Kaddish*. A *Yarzeit!* A mitzvah. *Succah.* Something! At least you'll have some Jewish content. Don't worry about what people will think. It's the in thing to do—but now.

12. Be Strong

Synagogues enact a unique ancient ceremony whenever they conclude the Torah reading of one of the Five Books of Moses. The entire congregation stands and in unison publicly recites, "Be strong, be strong, and be strengthened" *(Hazak, hazak, v'nithazaik).*

This proclamation seems peculiar. The Jewish community has accomplished something of value. They have completed the reading (and study) of one of the books of the Bible. They deserve to be praised for their efforts, "Congratulations," the chanting of "Mazel Tov," would appear more suitable than the phrase customarily said.

Also, the statement "Be strong" suggests a need for encouragement. One tells a depressed person to be happy and a weak person to be strong. The phrase alludes to the need for a status transformation: a change of character. But why is this so? Why at the zenith of achievement is the synagogue community considered so dispirited that it must be charged with a call for vigor?

Most do not recognize that success breeds a special emotional instability. The process of completing a difficult goal generates an overpowering urge of excitement. Creativity is present. The mind is clear. An inner-directed competitive spirit crystallizes extra energy and power. The person is transformed to a finely honed being whose physical and mental faculties are working in harmonic unity.

Indeed, when the goal is finally within sight, the excitement bolsters effort. Extraneous issues become disregarded. Time

33

and sleep lose their importance. The goal and the man become one. Then "Mazel Tov"—success is achieved. The euphoria is simply splendid.

But then the adrenalin is lost. The human machine slows down. Normal, tedious, mundane activities take over both mind and soul. The excitement is transitory. Back to normal life. What a letdown! At this moment the success is history. The achiever is dispirited. He may even be burned out. He needs a new fire, a new goal, a new activity. But is it worth it?

So the Jew calls out, "Be strong, be strong, and be strengthened." Success should generate new goals.

Achievement should be the basis for greater strength, not for depression. Be strengthened, Jewish synagogues; use your success to breed greater attainments. Onward! climb—build, grow.

The Jewish community cannot rest upon its laurels. One cannot walk backwards into the future. Achievements in Jewish education (for example), though remarkable, must be improved. The Jewish commitment can never be "burned out." It must and will go from strength to (greater) strength.

Jews have achieved remarkable attainments. They have endured a Holocaust. They crystallized the State of Israel. What now?

The synagogue drama is a charge to all Jews for all times. "Jews, be strong. We have accomplished great moments in history. Be strong, for the future will yet be better."

13. Parental Obligations to Children

Jews are mandated not only to perform mitzvot by themselves, but to so educate their children in Torah that upon reaching the age of maturity the children will have the ability to observe the laws and customs of our people. This process is called *chinuch*. Yet, how is this to be accomplished? Is it sufficient to merely acquire a teacher for a child or to register the child in school? A brief analysis of an halachic theory of Rashi's adds a unique nuance of meaning to this concept.

The Mishnah rules that minor children are not required to recite the *Shema*. Rashi contends that the Sages never imposed an obligation upon fathers to instruct their children in this mitzvah because (the fathers) are not at home together with their children at the periods of time when the *Shema* should be chanted (*Berachot* 20a). In other words, the fathers were generally not at home when the children would wake up in the morning or retire in the evening, the normal times for the *Shema*.

What is problematic is that parental presence appears to be crucial to the process of *chinuch*. Yet, of what significance is such parental presence? Children should be taught the technical knowledge for the proper performance of mitzvot and then should comply with the requirement. Why is it necessary for fathers to be visibly present during the performance of mitzvot by their children?

• It is apparent that Rashi is suggesting that *chinuch* is much more than the acquisition of Jewish knowledge. It is the verifi-

35

cation of a father that his child is actually performing the mitzvah accurately. It also gives the child confidence knowing the personal attention and interest of a parent. Such an obligation cannot be delegated to others. Each parent must see with his own eyes how his child is progressing. It is not enough to hear reports that his child has the ability and requisite skills but to see how his child realizes his potentiality by performances.

• An alternative option is that *chinuch* requires the children to emulate the role model of their parents. Children must see how their parents observe mitzvot: How their mother kindles the Sabbath lights, how their father prays, how their parents observe Chanukah. Jewish education must not be learned in a vacuum of family observance. As a result, the parental presence is required not as a mean of certifying observance but as an educational technique to bolster the inculcation of traditional values.

Thus, the essence of *chinuch* is personal involvement with our children for the cause of Torah.

14. *Jewish Leaders or Parents*

What makes a good Jewish leader? Is it pizzaz, style, sophistication, and charisma? Though these items are manifestations of form without content, they simply cannot be downgraded as valueless. They have a function. They serve as vehicles for success, fame, and influence—all of which are goals important for leaders. Yet they are the accouterments of popular leadership, not traits essential for definition.

Is it knowledge, compassion, initiative, piety, oratory, and bravery? Again, all such items are important to Jewish leaders but too vague and general to define the basic core of character.

It is of interest that our great teacher Moshe provides in Scripture the inner trait essential for Jewish leaders. Moshe complains about the bickering internal strife of the Jewish people. Why must he be so burdened with such a people. "Have I brought them forth, that Thou should say unto me: Carry them in thy bosom as a nursing father carrieth the nursing child" (Numbers 11:12).

In other words, Moshe contends that the Almighty requires a Jewish leader to be a parent.

Why a parent?

A parent cares for his children. That is his nature. Activities or services that he would decisively refuse to provide to a stranger, he will willingly serve to his child. Insults and embarrassment that would not be tolerated from a stranger will be totally overlooked when they emanate from a young child.

The infant is the responsibility of the parent. No decent parent would presume that a child could grow or mature without parental care, love, and support. Parent and child cannot be divorced. Each is part of the other. So too the Jewish leader and the Jewish community. Leadership is not a job, a profession, or a contractual relationship—it is parenthood.

Rav Yisrael Salanter tells the following tale. A rabbi had a son who lived not up to his ideals. The son was neither as religious nor as knowledgeable in Torah as the father would desire. Yet the rabbi had a student who was like a son. This student was all that one could wish for in a child. He was good, creative, pious, and learned in Torah. One day all three went for a ride in a boat. As inclement weather developed, the son and the student were washed into the water. Both stretched their hands to the rabbi for help. The rabbi knew he could only save one of them. Which one was it to be: the wayward son or the wonderful disciple? Logic might suggest that the rabbi would save the brilliant student. Yet the deep-seated subconscious love of a parent for a son overruled the dictates of reason. The father saved his son. Parenthood can be denied consciously but never rooted out of the subconscious emotions. The love of a parent for a child is a symbiotic relationship of togetherness. That is what a Jewish leader is. Everything else is but the veneer of social relations. A good Jewish leader is a spiritual parent surrogate. No—not a surrogate. He is a real parent. That is the test of leadership.

15. Training for Giving

Judaism values scholarship and piety. Those who excel in each of these spheres are afforded great homage and deference. The scholar-teacher rabbi serves as a model for leadership. Simultaneously, the mystic tzaddik rebbe is a source of inspiration for devotional experiences.

Yet Torah cannot be acquired without a guide, a teacher (a rebbe). There is a necessity for an existential dynamic relationship with a teacher to excite the mind, train logic, and guide the student in the path of self-study. It is almost impossible to achieve stature in Torah knowledge without such a personal relationship with a rabbi-teacher. So, too, with piety. One does not become a mystic overnight or simply through the study of books. Some master is necessary to set the aura and guide the sensations of the soul. This is what *mesora* (tradition) is all about. An actual person must personally teach the truth of Torah.

The Talmud says that Jewish life is based upon three pillars: Torah, religious service (prayer), and loving-kindness (*Avot* 1:2). Now, if a teacher is necessary for the proper acquisition of Torah and prayer, should it not be vital for the development of "good deeds"? That is, one should need a teacher (a rebbe) to become a master of kindness. One cannot crystallize a proper appreciation for charity and/or *chesed* (kindness) without someone who serves as a model to inculcate proper means and methods, and attitudes of kindness.

Scholarship requires the effort of training and research. Piety

39

is a result of self-examination and thought. Should not "kindness" also require training?

Yet how is this to be accomplished? Does affluence automatically confer knowledge of giving and care to a person?

This suggests a unique obligation of parents, teachers, and leaders. Love of knowledge is imbued to children at an early age. So, too, should be the act of giving to others. Some concrete examples:

• Children should be trained that to give to others is a daily commitment performed with the same regularity as eating and sleeping. Parents should have a *pushke* (charity box) and daily should not only give themselves but have their children put money therein. Even a penny a day. But every day. No day should pass without some (even token) form of giving. A child so accustomed will recognize the importance of charity.

• The positive virtue of sharing must be discussed in the home. Stories of Jewish philanthropy must be extolled. Folklore heroes must be related with pride. The art of Jewish kindness must be valued with the same vigor extended to scholarship, financial acumen, or other endeavors.

• Jewish *chesed* (kindness) must be noted as an important trait above and beyond charity. Indeed, kindness differs from charity in three ways: kindness is to both rich and poor (charity only to the poor); kindness may be with warmth, solace, words, and love (charity is with material benefit); kindness may be an act of honoring those no longer with us (charity is only to those who are alive).

• Parents must be careful not to express negative statements about the process of charity collection or the suitability of collectors or recipients. Children must grow up with the attitude that parents are proud to give. Realistic negative overtones must be submerged as an educational technique.

• The fact that charity to the poor may pragmatically lessen funds available for luxury should be discussed within the family as a trait of Jewish nobility. Jews do not live merely to cater to their desires.

• Living models of Jewish philanthropy must be sought out. They may not necessarily be scholars of Torah or the most devotional of Jews. But they must be masters of the art of *chesed*. They must serve as teachers—as those who teach us how to give with dignity, love, and joy. There are such men and women of *chesed* available. They should be our models for action and the enhancement of our children's lives.

I, for one, maintain that they deserve the homage granted to the best of our people. For who can deny that they are the giants of our age?

16. A Good Man

It is said that "a good man is hard to find." Perhaps it's because the term itself is difficult to define. What is a good man?

The prophet Isaiah maintains that the role of man is to "cease to do evil and to learn well" (*chidlu haraya, limdu haytav*, Isaiah 1:16–17).

Yet Rashi alters the literal translation of the text by contending that the latter phrase means *l'haytiv* "Learn to do good." In other words, a good man may be noted not by his inherent quality of character but, rather, by the practical manifestation of his good deeds. A good man does good for others. He is not selfish.

Thus, anyone who cares only for himself or his personal needs lacks goodness. The good man must be "other-directed," his basic concern must be a conditioned desire to serve people other than himself.

Yet the word "good" is ambiguous, for its impact is relative to diverse conditions. What is good to one person may be a calamity to another.

The Talmud (*Bava Batra* 21a) states that Yehoshua ben Gamla was to be always remembered for goodness (*latov*), for if not for him, Torah would have been forgotten from Israel. In his day those who had fathers were taught Torah (by their fathers), while orphans had no one to teach them Torah. As a result, Yehoshua ben Gamla instituted compulsory education for young children throughout each village and town of ancient Judea.

Thus, Yehoshua ben Gamla is classified as a good man for his deed in furthering Jewish education. What was it specifically that he accomplished? His concern was for those who could not care for themselves. Yehoshua ben Gamla was apprehensive over the ignorance of orphan children. Such children had no means of acquiring Torah knowledge. He, therefore, instituted compulsory schooling for all children in order that orphan children would be guaranteed an education equal to others; for in the classroom all children are peers.

This then is a good man. It is a person who assumes responsibility for the needs of those who cannot serve themselves. In addition, he sustains the need in a manner of dignity and equality. No wonder such a person is hard to find.

17. Faith vs. Action

Is faith an obstacle to action? Is the use of human intervention symptomatic of "no confidence" in God's powers of salvation?

Scripture states: "It is better to take refuge in the Lord than to put confidence in man" (Psalms 118:8).

This suggests that the man of faith should rely solely upon the will of God. In times of crisis one should utilize the vehicle of prayer to alleviate problems. War, battle—all human actions to achieve meaningful political and social results—may be the instruments of nonbelievers. "God will help" should be the motif of the religious personality. Is this Judaism? Is this the moral mandate of religion?

If so, then community activists should retire. The means of securing freedom for Soviet Jewry should be mass demonstrations of prayer. PLO problems? Terrorists and anti-Semites? All can be eliminated if the Jew would only truly pray and put his confidence in the hands of God.

There are those today who fervently subscribe to some aspects of this ideology as it pertains to Israel. They believe that the true Jewish state will only be manifested in the era of the Messiah. Human actions to support and sustain the State of Israel are antireligious acts that suspiciously manifest a lack of trust in God and His holy timetable for salvation. To the nonbeliever such a philosophy gives strength to their noninvolvement with religious values. It enhances their conviction that religion itself is an outmoded relic that withholds progress and subscribes to a "do-nothing" orientation for life.

This is a classic example of setting up religion as a "straw man" and then denigrating it for displaying unpopular features.

The truth is that divine salvation is not antithetical to human intervention. Just the contrary. The popular idiom that "God helps those who help themselves" is indeed a basic axiom of Jewish religious life. There is even a special Jewish nuance that shapes the pragmatic contours of this concept.

Man must endeavor to utilize all proper means available to achieve desired results. He cannot and should not rely simply upon his faith in divine intervention as a precondition for effort.

No less a sage than the Vilna Gaon contends that God does not help man unless God determines that man has tried and utilized every means available to him. This suggests that when the Almighty notes (and only God has such powers of discernment) that man has no other human recourse—that he has tried everything; that no other effort can be sustained or channel of action maintained—then, and only then, does the divine salvation crystalize. (See commentary, *Sukkah* 52b.)

Thus, one cannot rely upon divine help as long as man can yet achieve results. Indeed, our God knows whether we have yet other potential efforts. Even should we believe that there is nothing left for us to do, God knows whether this is so. The man of faith must, therefore, be a champion of action; for he knows that only after all has been attempted will his God not forsake him. Thus faith spurs action and negates sole reliance upon prayer.

Man must rely upon himself. He prays for the ability to truthfully recognize the extent of his own capacity. He asks God to bless his efforts. But if all fails, he knows that the ultimate help will come from God, not other men.

"It is better to take refuge in the Lord than to put confidence in man" (Psalms). The Gaon of Vilna notes (see his commentary on Psalms) that the Hebrew word for "refuge" is *cheesayon*, while the biblical term for "confidence" is *bitachon*. The distinction is as follows: *Bitachon* relates to the confidence one has that another will fulfill a commitment to do something in one's behalf. *Cheesayon* refers to the trust that one has that another will come to one's aid even without a special promise to do so. Scripture, therefore, is saying, Better to rely on the salvation of God, even without a specific vow to help, than to sustain confidence in the aid of men, even though they promise to so provide.

In other words, when all fails; when no other effort can achieve proper results; when everything has been attempted; the ultimate salvation is from God, not man. But God awaits our actions. We must strive. We must not fool ourselves into inactivity. This is what faith demands. This is the role of the believer.

18. Judging Others

How does one judge another person? What are the criteria for assessing character and moral standards?

The scriptural Book of Proverbs suggests a social measuring rod for such assessments. It states, "The refining pot for silver, and the furnace for gold, and *man according to his praise*" (27:21).

1. Rashi notes that the true essence of silver and gold is tested through the refining process. So too is the character of man. It is gauged by his reputation. Public opinion provides the valuation of one's achievements. Ask people about a certain person. Hear what they say. Listen to the qualities they extol. Man will be known by his praise.

This theory has basic limitations. Not all acts are known to the public. Not everyone even desires to disclose values to others or charitable deeds to the social arena. What public opinion does is to assess general recognition for integrity and services rendered. It relates the level of appreciation for the known values of a person. In addition, public opinion may reveal more about the standards of the community than about the individual it presumes to judge.

A case in point: Rabbi Moshe Sherer, president of the Agudath Israel of America, once told me the following anecdote.

When HaGaon Rav Aaron Kotler died, a call was made to the *New York Times* to provide a reporter to be at the funeral. "Who was Rabbi Kotler?" asked the *Times*. "He was the great *rosh yeshivah* (dean) of the yeshivah in Lakewood, New Jersey," was the response. "A rabbi in Lakewood, New Jersey? The *New York Times* doesn't cover the funerals of small-town rabbis." "No, you don't understand. Rabbi Kotler was a Torah great. A teacher and Jewish leader revered by Jews all over the world. He was the greatest rabbi of our times," came the agitated reply. "Hmm, how long was Rabbi Kotler in America? You say over two decades? We'll check the morgue and respond to you shortly."

"Morgue" is newspaper terminology for the back files of old issues of the paper. After a brief period, a call was received. "Hello, this is the *New York Times*. We've checked our files. Rabbi Kotler was not ever mentioned. Consequently, we will not send a reporter to his funeral. Why? For a rabbi to live over two decades in America and not to be listed even once in the *New York Times* shows that he could not be of any significance. Sorry."

The next day close to 75,000 Jews assembled to mourn the passing of Rav Aaron Kotler (z.l.), their beloved rabbi. To the world of Torah, Rav Aaron was the rabbi's rabbi. The greatest of the great. To the *New York Times*, not important. Whose values do the pages of the *New York Times* reflect?

2. Rabbenu Yona suggests an alternative interpretation of the verse "and man according to his praise." He contends that Scripture does not maintain that a man is to be assessed by his public reputation. No, not at all. The Bible is rather saying that a person's character may be known according to what the individual himself praises and esteems. In other words, do not seek information from others—but from the person himself. What does he praise? What values are important to him. What traits are valuable to himself. Does he extol morality and philanthropy? Or does he lavish praise upon materialism or immoral activities?

HaGaon Rav Hutner (*rosh hayeshivah,* Rabbi Chaim Berlin Rabbinical Academy) noted two concrete examples wherein such valuations suggest unique insight into character.

A. Two people. One learns Torah constantly. The second is a businessman. The first, the student, gives *kavod* to men of affluence but disregards rabbinic scholars. The second, the businessman, is in awe of religious leaders and shows no reverence to men of affluence. Though, in one measure, the student has greater Torah knowledge than the businessman, in terms of another measure, appreciation for Torah, the businessman is on a higher level than the student.

B. Two people in middle age. One, a student of Torah, regrets his sole preoccupation with Torah knowledge. He wishes he had devoted his concern to business rather than Torah. The second person is a businessman. He is sorry that he selected a secular occupation rather than Torah learning as a career. Even though the first person is a talmudic master, and the second is ignorant of Torah learning, the second man manifests a greater, finer, and more appreciative role of Torah than the professional student. This is but a higher example of Rabbenu Yona's interpretation of "and man [is known] according to his praise" (*Pachad Yitzchok, Purim* 1:3).

An additional viewpoint may be gleaned from the following. Proverbs states, "Let another man praise thee, and not thine own mouth" (27:2). Yet the Talmud rules that in a situation wherein one is unknown, self-praise is permitted (*Nedarim* 62a). As such, when a person seeks to identify himself, assess the quality of praise he lauds himself. How does a man describe himself? Does he state that he is a rabbi, a religious Jew, or a great rabbi and a saint. Such self-descriptions, indeed, test the mettle of character.

3. Rav Hutner suggests a third interpretation of the verse "a man according to his praise." He contends that people may be noted by a general characteristic: namely, are they basically positive or negative in relationship to others? Do they generally

lavish praise or scorn? Are they people who seek to compli-
ment others, or do they denigrate the accomplishments of
others? Thus, the integrity of a man may be reflected in the
nature of his general orientation toward praise. It's true. Some
can never laud the attainments or character of another person.
It's their nature to denigrate and scorn.

To judge another person, perhaps all three qualities should
be forged into a unified measuring rod. A man's nature may be
assessed by three tiers of judgement: reputation, values, and
character. Hopefully, all three may grant some understanding
of what a person is all about.

19. Overconfidence:
A Lesson in Humility

It is said that life itself is the greatest of all teachers. How true. The most intense manual on character development, the most sacred volume of ethics, or even the most profound and exciting lecture cannot match the impact of personal experience. A case in point.

Some time ago I attended a Ph.D. program in sociology at Fordham University. This institution was (and is) the intellectual bastion of the Jesuit movement in New York City. A requirement was proficiency in two foreign languages. I informed the chairman of the Graduate Department that I would like to use Hebrew as one of my foreign languages. He immediately retorted that such a selection created a problem. The university had a number of prepared written tests in French, German, Spanish, Russian, and even Chinese. There was, however, not available any such exam in Hebrew. In fact, no one had ever used Hebrew at Fordham University to meet the language requirement. After I protested—contending that the study of ancient Hebraic texts was a vital, integral part of my thesis—he relented by noting that he would request formal permission for such an exam from the chairman of the Graduate School.

Several weeks later I was shown a letter received from the chairman of the Graduate School which said something to the following effect:

"It is normal to expect peculiar requests from the Sociology Department. But this is really a winner.—Cohen? (Simcha?) Hebrew? Sociology? Fordham? This is quite an incongruity. But, we will create a special Hebrew exam for Cohen. He had better know his material. Please have him contact Father Fitzmyer, the chairman of the School of Theology." So I complied and forthwith contacted the good Father Fitzmyer.

I still remember the conversation.

"Hello, this is Jacob Cohen. It is my understanding that you will set up an exam for me in Hebrew."

"Yes, I've been told about you. How long would you like to prepare for the exam? Is a year sufficient? Or would you need more time?"

"Oh, no. I don't need so much time at all. I would really like to take it almost immediately, providing, of course, that your schedule so permits."

"How soon is immediately?"

"This week or even next week at the latest." (The day of the conversation was Wednesday.)

"How about Monday morning, at 9 a.m.?"

"Oh, that's really great. Thank you."

"See you Monday."

"Bye."

I felt very confident about the exam. I was an ordained Orthodox rabbi and quite confident of my years of training, studying, and analyzing texts in the original Hebrew language. What could a Father Fitzmyer really know? So I didn't even study. I didn't prepare in any way for the exam. Even emotionally—I was calm and self-assured.

The proficiency tests in foreign languages were generally a 30- to 45-minute written exam. Students were provided with selections to translate in order to manifest an ability to do research in a language other than English. So why should a rabbi have any qualms over a test in Hebrew? Especially if the exam is prepared by a gentile. A priest, no less.

Monday morning I met with Father Fitzmyer, a distin-
guished-looking priest enrobed in a cassock. "Would you prefer a written or an oral exam?" he asked.

"Whatever is most convenient for you," I responded.

"OK. We'll have an oral exam. Open up the Bible and
translate some sections from the Old Testament."

This was too good to be true. Old Testament? What a cinch!

"Please open the Bible to the Book of Job," he said. Oh, my!
Here come problems. Job is the most difficult text to translate.
It's replete with strange nouns and unfamiliar words. What a
test I received. After almost four hours of relentless, gruelling,
probing questions pertaining to roots of Hebrew words, complex conjugations of biblical grammar, Bible history, and com-
parative interpretations, torrents of perspiration streaked over
my brow. I had had it. I looked up at him with mental and
physical exhaustion intertwined with shock as he said, "Your
Hebrew is not too bad—but your English is atrocious." What?
He then asked me if I had ever read the entire Bible, from
beginning to conclusion, in English. When I replied in the
negative, he noted. "That's quite evident. You seek the *p'shat*
(the meaning) rather than an aesthetic translation. I have read
and mastered seventeen English translations of the Bible. The
Bible has a poetic beautiful resonance to its words. This elo-
quence of expression should be maintained when translated.
But I guess it's your training in *p'shat* that prevents you from
such a translation."

I couldn't believe what I had heard. *P'shat*? From a Father
Fitzmyer? He then mentioned that Aramaic was his forte, not
Hebrew—and that he was one of the translators of the Dead
Sea Scrolls. I couldn't help myself, so I asked, "How many men
are there like you in America?"

"Oh, there are at least a handful of us here." My *mazel!* Out
of thousands of colleges and universities and tens of thousands
of professors—I had to be destined to be tested by one of the
few true, great scholars, a giant in the field of translation. As I

blurted out the above expression, he looked at me with a twinkle in his eye and said, "Well, you did appear to be somewhat overconfident."

How right he was. I never met this man again. Yet I have never forgotten the incident. Yes, I passed the exam. Hopefully, I learned a lesson, too.

20. *Kavod: A Chronic Ailment*

Kavod—honor—is a status most seek to attain. It is a sense of esteem; a form of recognition for unique qualities. It manifests that others appreciate one's inner worth.

Yet it could also be an ailment that corrodes moral sensibilities and beclouds ethical judgments.

The Talmud notes that it is a special mitzvah to care for the needs of those who lose their wealth. They must be restored to their previous status of dignity. Hillel the elder would provide such people with a horse to ride upon as well as a slave to run before them. Once he could not acquire a slave, so he himself ran before one who had lost his wealth (*Ketubot* 67b).

This tale is bizarre and difficult to understand. The poor man came from good stock. He once had been a distinguished member of the community. He knew that Hillel was the spiritual leader of the Jews—a man extolled for piety, humility, as well as vast scholarship. Hillel was not a slave. So how could he permit Hillel to provide for him such obviously low service? How could he allow the *nasi* of the Jews to behave like a servant? Also, serious questions must be directed to Hillel himself. Why did he so lower himself? Are the wild whims and outrageous pipedreams of fools to be afforded respect? Hillel represented the *kavod* of the Jewish people. He had no right to denigrate himself.

HaGaon HaRav Chayyim Schmuelevitz (*rosh yeshivah*, Mir, Jerusalem) suggested that this case epitomized the havoc generated by a chronic, irrational passion for *kavod*. The poor person was totally sane and rational in everything except when it came to *kavod*. *Kavod* blinded his judgment. The desire for *kavod* made him lose contact with reality. His sickness made him actually believe that he deserved that Hillel should dance before him. Hillel also made a judgment. As a giant of Jewish law he determined that this man's sickness for *kavod* was so great, so permeating his existence, that it had become a life threatening problem *(pikuach nefesh)*. As such, Hillel danced before him as a means of theoretically saving his life.

The desire for *kavod* can become a chronic condition. It increases with age. As physical abilities dissipate, love of *kavod* increases. Once one is afflicted with this ailment, very few cures are known.

There is, however, a preventative therapy—to endeavor throughout life to benefit other people. To seek their honor. To elevate their status; to demonstrate their worthiness in life. Even to family members the esteem of others is commendable. The more one seeks to ennoble another's status, the less one is inclined to develop an inflated ego. The simple formula is as follows: Giving *kavod* is a mitzvah, seeking *kavod* is a sin.

21. Names Hurt

"Sticks and stones will break my bones, but names will never hurt me." So goes a rhyme learned by most in childhood. It is a means of teaching children character and pride. The negative names others cruelly use to hurt or denigrate should not be allowed to inflict pain. They are but empty, meaningless gestures. People are not to be depressed by such words. Physical abuse is a problem to fear. Verbal abuse should have no impact upon a person.

The sentiments are noble but truly contrary to reality. Harsh verbal abuse can seriously hurt another. It can deflate ego, denigrate self-esteem, and depress character. It can be remembered for ages and cause the victim to harbor visions of revenge. In fact, to some verbal brutality is more onerous and painful than a physical attack. The humiliation crystallized can seriously alter a lifestyle.

It should be noted that Judaism classifies verbal brutality as a sin, a violation of biblical law. Scripture states, *V'lo tonu ish et amito* (Leviticus 25:17). Some translations of the Bible somehow miss the essence of the verse. The Jerusalem Bible (1980, Koren Tenakh) says, "You shall not therefore *defraud* one another." The Menorah Press edition of the Holy Scriptures (1957) and the Jewish Publication Society version (1947) state, "And ye shall not *wrong* one another." Yet it is not clear as to what specific wrongdoing the Bible prohibits. The Talmud rules that this verse condemns the verbal slighting of the feelings or sensitivities of another. One is prohibited to make reference to

57

a dubious past, to call someone jeering, nasty names, or even to arouse false hope, such as by asking the price of an item in a store that one does not intend to buy. Accordingly, Samson Raphael Hirsch accurately relies on talmudic tradition by poignantly translating the verse to mean, *"Ye shall not hurt the feelings* of one another."* Thus Scripture is translated to say what it means. Just as Shabbat is important, so too are the sensitivities of another. One is prohibited to steal. So too is it a crime to make a person feel badly. The Talmud considers such oral hostility as comparable to physical abuse.

The *Hiddushei Rim* (the noted leader of the Ger Chasidim) added a marvelous nuance of meaning to this verse. It is known that a Chasid is defined as one who performs above and beyond the minimum requirements of the law *(lifnim m'shurat hadin)*. The Torah prohibits hurting the feelings of another. That is the law. So what role is performed by the Chasid? The *Hiddushei Rim* notes that a Chasid seeks not to even hurt his own sensitivities and feelings. He too is a person.

22. No Shouting

The Talmud records, "It once happened with Hillel the elder that he was coming from a journey, and hearing a great cry [a sound of shrieking] in the city, he said: I am confident that this does not come from my house" (*Berachot* 60a).

Most people would be apprehensive; their anxieties would increase upon hearing such a sound of disaster. People are crying. Women are moaning. Children are screaming. Something terrible has occurred.

Why was Hillel so calm? How did he know that no misfortune or tragedy had taken place in his home?

Hillel was a modest man. He constantly downplayed his accomplishments. He never sought the accouterments of *kavod*. Consequently, it goes against his character to assume that he believed that his personal merits would guarantee him safety against disaster.

Rav Shlomo Kluger (citing the Maharsha) contends that Hillel had instituted in his household the moral principle to never shout or scream when faced with trouble. Even calamities must be accepted calmly. The fact that people were shouting was indicative to Hillel that his household was not involved, for his family never shouted (*Maamar Esther*, p. 80).

What a wonderful attribute to instill in all homes. No shouting. No screaming. No loud voices.

A noted Englishman is reputed to have told a friend who was yelling at him, "Your logical arguments do not improve as the volume of your voice increases." How true. Being loud doesn't mean being right.

Reference to this concept may be noted in the verse *Divrei chachamim b'nachat nishma'im*—"The words of the wise *b'nachat* are heard" (Ecclesiastes 9:17). The Hebrew word *b'nachat* means "quiet" and/or "joy." As such it may relate to either the first or the last phrase. Accordingly, there are two distinct interpretations.

1. "The words of the wise are heard" (i.e., accepted joyfully). People wish to hear the words of the wise; sage remarks are a joy for all.
2. "The words of the wise spoken quietly are heard." Even scholars must measure the volume of their remarks. People do not like loud shouting even when it emanates from wise men. Yet the same thoughts gently spoken will have a greater impact upon any audience.

The latter view was Hillel's rule. He trained his family to speak in a gentle, modulated fashion. To scream was not the role of the wise. To shout or yell, not the image of wisdom.

A family guided by such a principle certainly would not shriek at a calamity. Hillel was a gentleman. So too was his mode of speech. The wise Jew is gentle in speech. What a lesson for all to learn.

23. *A New Jewish Song*

Music expresses diverse conditions and emotions. It can both sadden and gladden our hearts. It crystallizes a sphere of dignity or an aura of enchantment. Accordingly, the phrase noted in the Siddur (prayer book) that "with a *new song* the redeemed people offered praise at the seashore" seems difficult to understand.

What is a new song? The statement refers to the "Song of Moses and Israel" chanted after the miraculous splitting of the Red Sea (see Exodus 15). Yet close scrutiny of Scripture does not disclose any unique aspect to this song. It was but a poetic expression of thanksgiving for salvation. Is that the definition of "a new song"?

Were not people prior to the Exodus happy? Did they not express their joy through the medium of song? Were there no national hymns of praise?

Two explanations:

• This was the first time in the history of the Jewish people that the entire nation sang in unison one song. The "newness," or uniqueness, was not the poetic phrases uttered but the totality of the singers. All Jews sang. This was not an example of a few or several segments of the population exhilarated. It was a model for Jewish happiness. It was unity through music. Though many had different experiences of agony and perceived distinctly personal sensations of freedom, all utilized the same song to express their feeling of thanksgiving. Accordingly, a new Jewish song is the music of all Jews. It is Jewish harmony.

61

• On the verse "This is my God and I will glorify Him," the Targum Onkelos commentary adds the phrase, "And I will build a sanctuary to the God of my fathers" (Exodus 15:2).

This suggests a unique role of commitment. Most people are happy when wonderful events occur. Their joy is an expression of happiness for the good that has transpired. The song they sing is a natural reaction of happiness.

Yet how many people sing because of the future? This is what the Jews at the Red Sea did. They sang their resolve to go to Israel and to build a Holy Temple. They were future-directed. They perceived the future—and it looked good. This is a new Jewish song. It is a song of faith and hope coupled with commitment. A desire to not rest upon the laurels of the past. A sensation that good tidings create commitments to alter the lifestyle of the present.

Where do we find such songs today? What unites our divergent and discordant elements? Is the future of Jewry a positive image? Let us seek out that which unifies Jews rather than what divides us. Let us hope for a future of togetherness. The role of Jews should be the development of a "new song." A song of unity and hope: for that is the first song of our people. That should be our song today.

24. A Jewish Achievement

Jews love to admire their own achievements. As a people committed to the meritocracy of knowledge, they lay claim to a wide variety of attainments. The winners of the Nobel Prize, it is noted, include a disproportionately high number of Jews. Does this not manifest the genius of the Jew? The ranks of world-renowned scholars in diverse fields of endeavor again are replete with Jews. Freud, Einstein, and Salk—are all Jews. Our people are leaders of philanthropy, science, literature, government, business, and the arts. We have made a dynamic impact upon society today and governments in the past. We feel that we are an asset to the world itself.

True, but all of the above were accomplished by individuals who happened to be Jews. There was no Jewish content in such feats. It is the genius of the Jew, not Jewishness per se, that is acclaimed.

What have we done as a people? What have we accomplished that is of concern to the Jew? What has the totality of our people achieved?

From a negative orientation, we share the pain of anti-Semitism. We suffered together the horrors of the Holocaust. We died in unity. But what about positive attainments?

It seems there is only one.

The singular accomplishment of our people as a nation in this century has been the establishment of the State of Israel. It was the only national (international) constructive accomplishment that was (and is) of a Jewish nature. Israel was not created solely by European Jews. Nor was it the province of the Sephardim alone. It became a nation because all Jews—those who went on aliyah and those who remained in the diaspora—dynamically united to crystallize the emergence of a Jewish state in the homeland of our forefathers. Religious and nonreligious worked together for a common goal. National egos were forgotten and ancient prejudices disregarded. Israel became a reality through the efforts of world Jewish activism.

Accordingly, Israel is so much more than another bastion of Jewish communal activity. It is qualitatively distinct from Jewish New York, Los Angeles, Paris, or London. It is a Jewish state. A government for Jews—led by Jews—in a Jewish homeland. No other Jewish community manifests such unique qualities. Where else are Jewish holidays national holidays? In addition, Israel is the creation of the totality of the Jewish world community. As such, every Jew in any area of world civilization has a stake in its success and growth. Israel was created by the world community of Jews—and whether we reside therein or not does not detract from its centrality to the Jewish people.

Israel marks the first and only instrumentality in our century wherein the Jewish genius was utilized to sustain a national Jewish achievement. As such, it deserves to be an integral concern of each Jew. It should be a greater source of pride than a Nobel laureate. It is the Jewish achievement of our age.

25. Hatikvah: The Song of Our People

To the common man, Hatikvah is the national anthem of Israel. It is to be sung with both pride and joy. It is a form of identification with Israel and its primacy to the Jewish people.

Yet those who ascribe to the yeshivah and Hasidic worlds as well as to halachic orientations absolutely refuse to sing this song. In fact, they make a point of eliminating it from any program under their auspices. Why? Are they against the State of Israel? Are they anti-Zionists?

A brief review of the history of the Hatikvah will shed light upon a view that is oft overshadowed and denigrated by emotional and popular concerns. (The following facts are culled from the *Encyclopaedia Judaica*.)

Naftali Herz Imber, during the latter part of the nineteenth century, composed the Hebrew poetic words—The Hatikvah. It is reputed that he was influenced by German and Polish lyrics. Subsequently, Samuel Cohen a resident of Rishon Le-Zion, set the words to a melody based upon a Moldavian-Romanian folk song entitled "Cart and Oxen."

The song became identified with Zionism at the Seventh Zionist Congress (Basle, 1905) when all present concluded the program with the singing of Hatikvah.

In 1933, at the Eighteenth Zionist Congress in Prague, it was formally declared to be the Zionist anthem. During the Mandate in Palestine, Hatikvah was viewed as the unofficial anthem. Indeed, in 1948 it was performed and sung at the ceremony celebrating the formation of the State of Israel.

Subsequently, it has been considered the anthem of the State of Israel. Yet there has not been a formal proclamation by the Knesset declaring Hatikvah to be the official anthem of Israel.

Who was Naftali Herz Imber? It is reputed that on his visit to Bombay, India, as well as Palestine, he was "wooed by missionaries and was later accused of apostasy." Even his friend Israel Zangwill believed that he had converted to Christianity to escape starvation. The latter part of his life was spent in America, wherein he was known to live in "squalor, misery and alcoholism."

Now here's the issue. The Jewish people are a holy nation. Our history is graced with martyrs who died rather than betray our religious beliefs. Our heritage is lined with rabbis, scholars, and pious Jews whose lifestyles were a model of moral rectitude. We are a nation that identifies with *kedushah*—holy sanctity. We are a people of the Torah.

Should this holy people use the words of an acknowledged alcoholic, reputed apostate, and immoral person as the theme of its national aspirations? Should a tune based upon "Cart and Oxen" be the song to stir the heart of a religious Jew? As a result, even those who love Israel and will fight to the death for its existence feel that the Hatikvah is repugnant to religious sensitivities and beliefs. Jews deserve a more suitable and significant anthem.

Today, the lay leaders of our people cannot tolerate such views. Anyone who refuses to sing the Hatikvah is stereotyped as an anti-Zionist. Some have even withheld funds from institutions that do not have the Hatikvah sung at their annual banquet. Others have castigated rabbis for not embracing the Hatikvah as the national anthem.

I, for one, sing the Hatikvah with pride. There are even times when the song evokes great positive emotions within me.

This does not mean that I approve of the morality of the composer or would not prefer an anthem written by a *tzadik*. There are many things that preferably should be altered yet are not forsaken; there are other facets of life that originally were denigrated yet subsequently became venerated.

An example: The Passover Seder commences with the phrase, "This is the bread of affliction that our forefathers ate in the land of Egypt." Yet Scripture specifically notes that the unleavened bread called matzah is a reminder that the Jews were rushing to leave Egypt and the bread had not time to rise (Exodus 12:39). In other words, matzah was not eaten while the Jews were in Egypt. It is a symbol of freedom and deliverance. Accordingly, this contradicts the statement that the bread of affliction (matzah) was eaten during the slavery.

The Vilna Gaon and others contend that matzah was the food provided for slaves throughout the bondage—it was a basic staple food item of the Jews. On the night of Passover the Jews baked bread. They wanted to taste real bread—not matzah. Yet, through a quirk of fate, that very night freedom was proclaimed. The Exodus was to commence. The bread could not be baked. There was no time to tarry. So matzah, which originally was denigrated as a symbol of servitude, became viewed as a message of freedom. The same matzah eaten only by slaves became transformed into the bread of freedom. Today we care not about the origins of Matzah. To us it is identified with liberty. It is now a Jewish symbol of freedom.

So too with the Hatikvah. Its roots may be clouded with non-Jewish origins and nonholy composers. So what!

For decades it was the clarion call for statehood. It stirred the emotions of Jews throughout the world. It united our people. Polish, Russian, German, English, Hungarian, Czechoslovakian, and American Jews all marched to its tune. All who envisioned a national homeland, a state, cherished its words—Hatikvah, the hope of the Jews. Jewish soldiers died with the words emblazoned in their hearts. It became the spirit of a reborn Israel.

Yes, the basic concern of the religious Jew is not necessarily "to be a free nation in our land." It is for the Messiah.

So Hatikvah is not the song of our rabbis. But it certainly is the theme of our people. It is the one song that all Jews sing. It is the one song that emotes national pride. It reminds us of the hordes of Arab soldiers, the displaced Jews of Europe, the homeland for the homeless, it is modern Israel. It is our song. It is our matzah. It is freedom. It is identified as our song. So let us sing it with pride.

26. Betar

Jews commemorate not only victories but also defeats. In fact, Tisha B'Av, a day of national calamity, records the devastating destruction of both the first and second Holy Temples. The Mishnah notes that the city of Betar was also destroyed and plowed asunder on Tisha B'Av. As such the martyrdom of the patriots of Bar Kochba's revolt (135 C.E.) is an integral aspect of our national mourning (*Taanit* 26b).

Yet, apart from sadness, the Betar defeat crystallized a special *berachah* (blessing) that was ritually added to the format of the Grace after meals, known as the *Birchat HaMazon*. The fourth *berachah* of *Birchat HaMazon* is classified as the *Hatov u'maitiv* blessing. The Talmud states that this blessing *Hatov u'maitiv*—"Who is good and bestows good"—was instituted in Yavneh with reference to those who were slain in Betar. For R. Mattena said: "On the day on which permission was given to bury those slain in Betar, they [the sages] ordained in Yavneh that 'Who is good and bestows good' should be said. 'Who is good,' because they did not putrify, and 'who bestows good,' because they were permitted to be buried" (*Berachot* 48b).

Such a *berachah* requires a clarification. Is it not strange to thank God that the destruction was not more terrible and onerous than, in fact, occurred? The words of the *berachah* connote a sense of goodness certainly lacking in defeat.

It is suggested that the sages perceived a benefit in the devastation, a benefit that had a long-range positive impact upon the status of the Jewish people. Accordingly, their words may have been symbolic of the following.

69

1. "The dead did not putrify." There was no stench or offensive aura to the martyrs' death. That is, they died with devotion, diligence, and bravery. No one could question their integrity. No one could denigrate their death. They were heroes to the end. The sages were proud of the martyrs, the soldiers, and the people. In defeat, the Jews knew that they had tried their best. They had acquitted themselves well.

2. "They were permitted to be buried." There are times when battles are won but war persists. The dead, somehow, are never buried. Their memories linger on. The image of the dead serves as a catalyst for revenge and further wars. The defeat at Betar buried the seed of revolt. The Jews knew that it was time to build the peace. No more insurrections. No more wars. This too is a blessing for a people ravaged by war.

In the world today, we Jews speak with pride over our fallen martyrs. They gave their best. But today our dead are not buried. No one lets them sleep in peace. They serve as cause, by our memories, for an ever reoccurring cry for revenge. Yes, there is peace. But a total *berachah* cannot be recited. For no one permits the dead to be buried and peace to prosper in its fullest capacity.

27. Blameless Hate (Sinat Hinam)

The talmudic sages discerned the imprimatur of divine retribution in the destruction of the First and Second Temples. Each era was noted as having manifested distinctively unique transgressions. The crimes of the First Temple were identified as idolatry, adultery, and murder. The period of the Second Temple was notorious for the sin of blameless hatred (*sinat hinam*). People hated one another for no just cause or reason.

Though the sin of blameless hatred was also evident during the epoch of the First Temple, it was a character flaw endemic to the leadership but not the common man (*Yoma* 9b). The logical implication is that, through the passage of time, the innocent hatred of one Jew for another filtered down from the leadership class to the average Jew. By the time of the Second Temple it was a widespread phenomenon. Most Jews simply hated each other.

Yet such an observation is difficult to comprehend. Humane concern and love are necessary ingredients to cement meaningful relationships. A community wherein all hate each other simply cannot exist or function properly. Were Jews so immoral, so hateful to each other?

Also, the Talmud records that during the Second Temple many were involved in the study of Torah, the performance of mitzvot, and the expression of loving-kindness (ibid.). How could such a generation be marked by blameless hatred? Didn't the Torah have a positive impact on their lives?

Rabbi Naftali Tzvi Hirsh Berlin (*N'tziv*), the famed dean of the Volozner Yeshivah, noted that murder was as rampant during the Second Temple as the First (see *Avodah Zarah* 8b). Yet a major orientation distinguished the crimes of the earlier period from those of the later. During the First Temple murderers knew that their acts were morally repugnant and reprehensible. They were aware that it was wrong to kill, to shed blood and take the life of another. At no time did they justify their sins as morally legitimate. They just did as they pleased with no fear of retribution.

During the Second Temple, however, murder was committed under the guise of a mitzvah. Again, no one contended that it was morally proper to murder an innocent person. Yet the common custom was to judge Jews guilty of capital crimes. An informer was to be killed. An apostate, an *apikores,* to be eliminated. A nonbeliever had to be destroyed. Each was deemed a legitimate death. It was the veneer of piety and religious purity that guided the hand of the executioner. Such deaths were not classified as murders but as religious penalties for heinous crimes. The people destroyed were viewed as deserving of punishment. Yet the basis for such vengeance, contends the *N'tziv,* was not altruistic religious piety, but, rather, blameless hatred of one Jew for another. It was hatred which swayed the severity of the punishments. Each case could have been viewed as a sin of passion rather than an act of apostasy. Each transgression could have evoked a compassionate response. It was the tragic seed of innocent hate that overwhelmed all concerns for justice (*Meromai Sadeh, Yoma* 9b).

Accordingly, the moral aura was rooted in hate—not love. Both leaders and common people became too enamored of their own self-inflated standards of religious purity. All who differed were to be destroyed for the sake of religious truth. It was a heightened form of Jewish inquisition.

Torah leaders became zealous parochial guardians of the faith. Charity and kindness were to be extended only to like-believing and like-observing Jews.

Thus, love and hate may coexist within the so-called champions of morality. All who seek vengeance in the name of God must examine their own inner souls. Is it based on the love of man, even one who disagrees, or upon the corroding distrust of blameless hate?

How relevant is the *N'tziv's* theory today! How easy it is to castigate all who disagree. The Jewish community is small in numbers. Our ranks have been decimated by enemies from without and apathy from within. Yet we are a nation of squabblers. Even within the Torah-observing community the wedge of disunity grows larger each year.

The Holy Temple was a physical entity as well as a symbolic unifying force. If destruction and dispersion were the result of blameless hatred, then "measure for measure" our redemption will be attained by "innocent love." Namely, love of all Jews— any type of Jew: Jews who agree with us and those who do not, religious as well as irreligious. Jews, rather than hate, divide, and punish in the name of God. Let us love, unify, and enhance people for the sake of religion. To err is human—to err because of basic moral love, that's the Jewish way.

28. An Elegy to Golda

On December 19, 1978—19 Kislev 5739—Golda Meir, the fourth Prime Minister of Israel, pioneer Zionist, and symbol of courageous Israel leadership, was laid to her eternal rest.

Death invokes a status transformation of mourning for relatives of the bereaved.

Chacham shemet, kol Yisrael k'rovav—when a Jewish leader dies, all Israel bonds together as one family for grief. It is no stranger who died. All Israel mourns for their mother, Golda.

Ayshet chayil me yimtzah (Prov. 31).

"A woman of valor—who can find?" *Chayil*—a soldier! Golda was a soldier; a disciplined warrior in behalf of her people and nation. *Me Yimtzah?* Where do we find another Golda?

Verachok mepneenim michrah.

"Her price is above rubies."

Jewelry, cosmetics, high fashion—not Golda's style, nor her values at all.

Batach ba layv baala.

"The heart of her husband does safely trust in her."

Golda was married to Israel. She held the trust of all Jewish hearts. The heart, feelings, pains, and hopes of even one Jew were her personal trust.

Gemalathu tov velo ra kal ymai chayeha.

"She doeth him good, not evil, all the days of her life."

To Israel—Golda's mate—in times of personal anguish or political retreat, never, never were her words and/or actions anything but good—not bad.

Therefore, *Kamu vanehah vayashruha, baala vay' halela.*

"Her children, yea her mate, rise up and call her praised."

Her children—all Jews, *her mate*—Israel. All are able to stand with greater pride because of her. Who does not speak her praise?

For Golda, all Israel is her family. Israel has lost its mother.

29. My Miracle

Folklore relates countless anecdotes of rabbis who performed miracles. Today, however, such wonders are reserved for a limited cadre of Chassidic rebbes and mystics. It is said, moreover, that modern pulpit rabbis simply lack the art of making miracles. Maybe so, yet I'd like to note one incident that but 100 years ago certainly would have been proclaimed as a wondrous feat.

In the summer of 1983, at the Great Synagogue in Jerusalem, one of the worshipers suffered a severe heart attack. Medical personnel were called and emergency procedures were performed to revive the person while the religious services proceeded. As the *kohanim* departed to have their hands washed, prior to *Birchat Kohanim* (the Priestly Blessing), a general state of confusion ensued. Some contended that since the heart-attack victim was in the last throes of life and it appeared as if he would die at any moment, the *kohanim* should preserve their purity by leaving the synagogue altogether. They had no right to remain for *Birchat Kohanim*.

My position was just the opposite. I firmly maintained that it was a mitzvah for the *kohanim* to remain in the synagogue to extend blessings, for such would heal the sick man. My rationale was as follows.

It is told that on the day that Rav Shlomo Kluger assumed his position as rabbi of Brod he was honored to serve as the *sandik* (Godfather) at a circumcision. When he arrived at the place where the circumcision was to occur, he was informed of a tragic situation. The father of the newborn son was dying. The local community had a custom that in such an occurrence they held off performing the circumcision until the very last moment of the day so that if the father died the new child would be granted the name of his own departed father.

Rav Shlomo Kluger refused to heed this custom and instructed that the circumcision ceremony should immediately take place. Subsequently, the father had a remarkable recovery and became quite healthy. Through the town Rav Kluger was acclaimed as a "miracle rabbi."

His rationale, however, had nothing to do with supernatural knowledge, but, rather, with talmudic logic. In Genesis, Rashi notes that the angel Raphael, who came to heal Abraham from his circumcision, was subsequently sent on a mission to save Lot from Sodom (Genesis 18:2). Yet this dual role of Raphael appeared bizarre to Rav Kluger. Did the Almighty lack angels in heaven that it was necessary to utilize Raphael to perform two functions? Perhaps he reasoned that Lot lacked sufficient personal merit to have an angel exclusively sent in his behalf. As a result, since Raphael had already been commissioned to help Abraham, while available he could also then save Lot. In other words, once an angel is present all who need help may be saved.

The sickly father was in a similar predicament; perhaps he did not have sufficient merit to warrant an exclusive angel charged with healing powers. To the extent that legend has it that Elijah the prophet is present at all circumcisions to heal the child, once he arrives he would heal also the sick father. And so it occurred.

My logic was that the heart-attack victim was in a similar plight. He was being divinely judged and lacked sufficient personal merit to be healed. He needed help. To the extent that the *kohanim* blessed the congregants, such blessing would extend also to the sick person. Perhaps this religious gesture would sway the scale in behalf of life. It was necessary to develop an aura of blessing for this man who could not crystallize it by himself.

One rabbi looked at me with incredulous wonder. "You mean you're going to make an halachic decision on the basis of a *baba maaseh* (a folklorish tale)?" "Yes," I said. "For I believe in the efficacy of prayer and the grace of *Birchat Kohanim*," and went with the others into the synagogue to pray. Of interest is that the heart-attack victim regained consciousness and lived. Now, is that (or is that not) a miracle?

30. Russian Voice from the Past

Life in America is simply great. Our major problems are to decide on courses of action from a wide variety of options. What type of profession to select? How to succeed? Whom to marry? Which house to buy? How to spend time? How to relax? How to make life meaningful? There's generally always a choice available to us. And most get bogged down in the details of procrastination of implementation of such decisions. We're so busy with ourselves that it's easy to forget our past, or even the pain that others experience. So, when I recently opened a letter from my uncle, an eminent economist and Russian scholar, I gasped at the contents he sent me. It was a translation of a letter in Russian from a family member long thought dead.

It said:

Dear brother twice removed
[the Russian word for "cousin" is "brother or sister twice removed"],

I am happy that in my declining years a fortunate accident afforded me the opportunity to discover that someone of our family survived after the bloody slaughter of the Second World War.

I will tell you briefly about the fate of my father, your uncle. He perished like a hero and, to me, his courage is a source of pride. He was taken hostage and asked to betray others—only he refused to become a traitor by prolonging his life at the price of the death of others. And so, in our out-of-the-way town, Frampol, they hanged him first. Before the execution he spoke briefly, predicting the inevitable doom of fascism and its cruelty.

After this tragic event, some 18,000 Jews from the entire area had been driven to station Yarmolinetz (if you still remember the names of our towns), and there brutally slaughtered—among them, my foster-mother, and older sister, Pearl, with her family. There stands now a monument to the victims.

So that's how Grand-Uncle Nachum died. I never knew. My oldest son was given the middle name Nachum, for my father, may he rest in peace, said, "Uncle Nachum was tall, strong, and never knew pain. He was always healthy." I guess he never knew pain in his life—but he died in pain, yet also in honor. The woman relative who wrote the letter is seventy-eight years of age. She had neither seen nor spoken to my uncle for over fifty years. Yet the pain and pride of her father's death so impacted her that it was vital to recall in the opening remarks of her first communication with the family in half a century.

American-born Jews were never confronted with Grand-Uncle Nachum's traumatic options. Our problems pale in comparison. Yet the story of his heroic death adds a nuance of importance to our so-called options for life. Perhaps it is now necessary to determine whether our decisions bring pride and joy to others or are simply selfish, ego-centered concerns.

Reb. Nachum's brother was my paternal grandfather, Ha-Gaon R. Shmuel, an internationally acclaimed scholar and author. His writings, the *M'danai Shmuel* (on Passover) and the *Minchat Shabbat* (on laws of Shabbat), were considered classic textbooks and guides for rabbis throughout Europe and are revered even to this day. R. Nachum—no one knew of him. His name is not even listed in records of rabbinic personalities. Yet, like his brother, he too was a teacher of Torah. R. Shmuel taught us how to live like a Jew. R. Nachum taught us how to die like a Jew. *L'chayyim*—R. Nachum.

31. Grading Students: A Parental Reaction

Parents want their children to do well in school. It's an inherent parental attitude which crystallizes even before a child attends nursery school. Some even say that this concern is generated when a child is born. Others contend that the idea germinates in the genes and comes to the forefront the moment conception is even contemplated. As a result, a child's school report card is a matter of grave importance.

My daughter stood before me carefully scrutinizing my facial expressions as I intently read her report card. "C," I said. My voice quivered and increased in volume. "C in grammar? How come?" As my brow wrinkled, I started to scowl and turned to look at her. My daughter, she knew me well. Before I had an opportunity to say anything else, she immediately told me not to worry at all. She was prepared with a ready-made response. "Oh, that, Dad. That's really a good mark. Our principal came to our class today and said that Mrs. X is one of the finest teachers in the entire school. But she has very high standards. So a C in her class is really comparable to an A by any other teacher."

As I listened to the explanation, I became angry—not at my daughter, but at the unfair marking system she appeared to morally accept. My mind raced back to a book I had read more than twenty-five years ago. A book entitled *Teacher in America* by Jacques Barzun. How strange it is that unfair practices have a tendency to persist and be clothed with the veneer of excellence. His position may be summarized as follows:

81

Any teacher who gives students low grades yet contends that due to extremely high standards of excellence such marks are to be viewed as equivalent to A's by others is blatantly unfair. Such a teacher would cry foul and be definitely annoyed if he gave someone $10 and received $5 for change with the explanation that this person's $5 was worth $10. Why? No one cares for an individual's personalized valuations of money. Such a standard cannot be imposed upon others. So too in a school situation. Students are judged by their marks. Honors, scholarship, and self-esteem are closely correlated to school grades. In fact, grade averages are the "bottom line" for standardized evaluations. No one teacher has the right to unilaterally alter the normal school grading system. Yes, it is the mark of a good teacher to make students strive for high levels of scholarship. But to impose a personal grading system for report cards is an affront to students and an act of arrogance.

As I looked again at the report card and thought of the above astute remarks, I had great compassion for my daughter as well as for all students. Children need not be subject to such discriminatory acts. It's hard enough to be motivated to learn and to satisfy demanding parents without being taught that arrogance is excellence and wrong is right. Principals should not take pride in such behavior but, rather, should root out such activity. The school is an institution not only for the education of children but also for the development of teachers.

It is said that life is unfair. So, it may be. But this does not mean that we should tolerate human wrongs when they may be rectified. Certainly in a school system. Fellow parents, let's stand up for student rights.

32. Bar Mitzvah Parties

Think Bar Mitzvah, and the image conjures up a gourmet's fantasy of parties and banquets. Hardly any Bar Mitzvah is celebrated without its concomitant festive meal. But why is this so? Is not a Bar Mitzvah a religious celebration? As such, it should be celebrated with special attention to religious concerns. The family, perhaps, should rededicate themselves to spiritual values which should be implemented by Torah sessions or charitable programs. Is not the banquet antithetical to the spirit of the occasion? It almost appears as if it was designed by caterers rather than by rabbis.

Yet it should be noted that the Bar Mitzvah party is not an innovation of modern life. It is rooted in our tradition, and is cited by ancient authoritative sages as a significant celebration of the Bar Mitzvah.

The Talmud notes that R. Yosef, who was blind, was troubled as to whether a person in such a condition was obliged to observe mitzvot. He said, "Now that I have heard R. Hanina's dictum that he who is commanded and fulfills the command is greater than he who fulfills it though not commanded, if anyone should tell me that the Halachah does not agree with R. Yehuda (who ruled that the blind are exempt from mitzvot), I would make a *yom tov* for the rabbis" (*Kiddushin* 31a). Rashi interprets the latter phrase to mean a banquet.

R. Shlomo Luria (1510–1574) derives from this the general rule that an initial obligation to observe mitzvot crystallizes a party celebration. The reason is that R. Yosef expressed a desire to have a banquet to celebrate his obligation to observe mitzvot. So too should transpire at a Bar Mitzvah. The thirteenth birthdate of a boy is a form of status transformation.

The Bar Mitzvah is the date wherein the boy assumes obligations to perform mitzvot in his own right. Accordingly, the party celebrates this new obligation comparable to R. Yosef's declaration. Though this suggests an ancient source, a rationale is yet necessary to comprehend its religious significance.

The Talmud records a debate as to the proper means to celebrate a holiday. R. Eliezar contended that *yom tov* should be totally devoted either to spiritual concerns (Torah) or to personal enjoyment. R. Yehoshua disagreed. He believed that *yom tov* should contain both elements—part spiritual, part personal, physical enjoyment (*Betza* 15b). Yet on Shavuot, the Talmud rules that there is no debate. Even R. Eliezar agrees that personal, physical enjoyment is necessary, for such a time commemorates receipt of the Torah on Mount Sinai (*Pesachim* 68b).

This citation is difficult to comprehend. Logic suggests just the opposite position. Since Shavuot commemorates Torah, on that day all physical enjoyment should be secondary to Torah. Jews should devote the entire holiday to Torah scholarship. Parties and banquets should have no place on a day of Torah. Religious aestheticism should prevail.

The meaning, perhaps, is that Torah was not given to angels but, rather, to human beings; to people with frailties and limitations. Torah does not mandate a monastic lifestyle. Life is to be appreciated, enjoyed, but sanctified. The physical pleasures are to be utilized to enhance life itself. Eat—but make a blessing to manifest an appreciation of God's gift. Joys of the world are to be controlled and uplifted.

The physical and spiritual spheres are to be integrated into a meaningful whole. The day commemorating the gift of Torah necessitates a recognition of the human quality of its essence. How better to do so than by participating in a party.

The Bar Mitzvah banquet is the concrete example of this concept. Each Bar Mitzvah boy is celebrating receipt of his personal Torah. As such, he commemorates the event with a festive meal, just as all Jews so observe on Shavuot. So let us enjoy the parties. But let us at least recognize that our goal is to uplift the material world rather than subordinate all values to the pleasure of the moment.

33. The Impact of Ritual Prayer

Modern exponents of religion characterize prayer as a personal, dramatic encounter between man and his Creator. As such, any restrictions pertaining to the mode or period of expression are viewed as hindering its spontaneity and counterproductive to a meaningful religious experience. Consequently, there has been a tendency to downgrade rabbinic ritual laws and to leave prayer to the individuality of the worshipper.

No one can deny that God accepts the spontaneous prayers of those who turn to Him when a unique mood or inspiration crystallizes the expression of spiritual emotions. Such prayers are always valuable. But they cannot replace the significant impact of ritually prescribed prayers recited at mandated periods of time.

Tradition requires the Jew to pray each day. Every morning, afternoon, and evening a portion of time must be devoted to a specific prayer. A prayer consciously neglected can never be replaced; just as a lost moment of time can never be restored.

This teaches us the importance of time. Not everything may be extended into the never-ending tomorrows of the future. Some matters must be done today—or never. Each portion of a day has the potential for meaningful pursuits. Once wasted, time cannot be retrieved. If we were sad yesterday, no action we take today can alter the fact of yesterday's sadness. Each moment is precious. A meaningful life is based upon the joy each moment can bring. Ritual prayer, therefore, impresses upon us the value of constructively utilizing time itself.

It also serves to discipline the mind of man. The Maharal, the sage and mystic of Prague, defined *tefilah* (the Hebrew word for "prayer") to mean *machshavah* ("thought") (see Genesis 48:11—Rashi). Prayer is thus an art that demands a systematic approach as well as an analytical understanding.

To really pray, man must think. He must endeavor to comprehend the ramifications of all that he says. He must involve himself in a process that necessitates self-understanding, obligations to others, and a relationship with God. Such a tripartite consideration is difficult to achieve.

Man's most human faculty is his mind, but at times he neglects to use it well. Therefore, to impress upon him the necessity of thinking each day, he is required to pray each day.

The Talmud says that if a man goes seven days without a dream, it is sinful (*Berachot* 55b). The meaning of this statement may be gleaned from another: "A man is shown in a dream only what is suggested by his own thoughts" (ibid.). This means that a person generally dreams at night what he thinks about by day. A person who doesn't dream for a week is a person who hasn't had a thought for a week. Such a person is sinful because he is neglecting his most fundamental quality.

Ritual law prescribes not only the time of prayer but also its format. The Jew is required, three times a day, to stand and say silently certain specific prayers, called the *Amidah*. Modern man rushes about in a never-ending web of routine activities; symbolically, the *Amidah* gives man a chance to stand still. A person who can't stand still cannot concentrate, cannot think, and certainly cannot pray. The *Amidah* provides the Jew with the proper aura for constructive thought. Still, silent, apart from the din and turmoil of the world, the Jew stands alone and thinks out his relationship with God, his fellow man, and himself.

But it is not enough to tell a person to think. What should he think about? Left alone, our minds will often wander aimlessly.

For this reason, ritual law prescribes the exact wording of our prayers. The Jew has his Siddur, his prayerbook, to guide his thoughts and direct his actions. His personal prayer is not sufficient unless he uses the language crystallized by rabbinic law. Each word, each phrase, each sentiment can inspire the worshipper to probe into the vast realm of sacred values and religious convictions. A wide range of human ideas and concerns are contained in the prescribed prayers; each person can concentrate on those that most express his personal interest and needs.

However, the primary concern of the worshipper should not be his personal problems, but those of his people at large. The *Amidah* prayers are phrased in the plural and refer to the community, rather than the individual (see Mishnaic commentary of Elijah, Gaon of Vilna, *Sh'not Eliyahu*, tractate *Berachot*, chap. 5, *Mishnah* 1). The quality of empathy is important for sincere and thoughtful prayer; a man must consider the needs of others. He must recognize that others also suffer, that he is not alone in his sorrows. Only after this fact is recognized may he add his prayers for his personal needs and concerns.

The fact that the prayers are phrased in the plural and apply to the community as a whole rather than the individual guides us to recognize the universality of all human concerns. Every person thinks his problems are unique, yet we all share in some form the entire range of human emotions and experiences.

Prayer, therefore, represents an opportunity to stand alone in dialogue with the Almighty, and at the same time silently to embrace the gamut of universal human emotions. When the Jew prays, he stands alone, yet he echoes the feelings of all men. Each man stands before his Creator as the spokesman for all men.

34. Birchat Kohanim

At each holiday, those Jews who trace their ancestry to Aaron the high priest and are categorized as *kohanim* bless the community. At such times it is customary for members of the congregation to thank the *kohanim* and to wish them well for their blessings. This expression of appreciation requires an explanation. *Kohanim* are not requested to voluntarily bless the people. They are commanded to do so. Just as all Jews are required to put on tefillin and observe Shabbat, *kohanim* are obliged to bless the community. No one ever thanks an individual Jew for observing Shabbat. Why then are *kohanim* thanked for their blessings?

The response is that the Torah mandates a blessing but does not direct or specify the attitudinal role of the *kohan*. There are many forms of a blessing. It may be recited as an empty ritual, without feeling, or as a true concern with meaning and love. The format of the *bracha* states that the blessing should be *b'ahavah*—with love. This emotional dimension was not mandated by the Bible. This concern is a voluntary, discretional element granted by the *kohanim*. The *kohanim*, therefore, are thanked not for their observance of the mitzvah but for their personal enhancement of the blessing by garbing it within the aura of love.

35. Permissible Envy

It is wrong to be envious. As *Pirke Avot* says, "Who is wealthy? He who is happy with his lot" (chap. 4, Mishnah 1). Envy is thus a violation of this dictum. It is a source of irritation which corrodes moral sensitivities and depresses normal satisfactions. It can be a disease that eats away the roots of harmony and stimulates contention and strife. Woe to the person who is constantly envious of others. Such a person is never satisfied, never happy. He is always confronted with new obstacles to overcome. As such, envy is a trait to be denigrated, to be rooted out from our moral concerns. It is no wonder that envy is included in the traits that drive a man from this world (*Pirke Avot* 4:21).

Yet traditional sources suggest that envy has a positive functional role. In discussing why the menorah is located in the Bible adjacent to the sacrifices brought by the leaders of the tribes, Rashi cites the following midrash: Aaron, the high priest, was jealous that the tribe of Levi was not honored by being included in the roster of sacrificial portions brought by the leaders of the other tribes. God told him, "Do not be concerned, for you, Aaron, will be responsible for the care of the menorah" (see Rashi, Numbers 8:2).

In other words, Aaron was not reprimanded for his envious attitude. He was not punished for overt jealousy but, rather, was appeased by the granting of an additional exclusive ritual. Why?

Perhaps, envy is not a morally repugnant trait. No, it is not the attitude which is condemned but, rather, the object of its attention.

One should not covet another's wife. Material gain and affluence should not generate envy. In these spheres of interest a person should be content with his personal possessions. Yet in the realm of intellectual activity and spiritual growth, perhaps envy should be a natural catalyst for self-betterment. Man should not be content with the kindness he expresses. He should not be satisfied with the knowledge he has. Viewing the charity others give should serve as a motivating envious challenge to improve personal actions. One should not be satisfied with one's moral development. Look at others. See how they overextend themselves to serve the poor and the needy. Be envious of their ability to serve God and man. Such envy is not a crime. No, perhaps it is a mitzvah. But please do not confuse the goals. Jealousy of material gain by others is not the goal of man. Kindness, greatness, stature, and knowledge—these are permissible enviable roles. Envy Torah, not money; kindness, not clothes; knowledge, not cars; charity, not homes. As Browning the poet so eloquently stated, "Ah, but a man's reach should exceed his grasp."

36. In Defense of Covering the Jewish Head

I cover my head. This practice is so much a part of me that I never leave my home without a hat firmly placed on my head. It's me. This is not a personal quirk of attire nor an idiosyncrasy of misplaced fashion. It's so ingrained within me that even here in sunny, leisureland, informal Los Angeles, I still wear a hat.

What's so surprising to me is that I now stand out in the crowd. I'm the man with the dark hat. You can locate me anywhere.

But why should this be so? Why don't people wear hats?

An essayist recently theorized that President Jack Kennedy devastated the hat industry. He alone, more than anyone else, made the uncovered head a symbol of youth and vigor. To wear a hat was to be old-fashioned and conservative. Just look at the young President Kennedy. Observe how dynamically he stood upright in the Washington cool air. Note the hue of snow tinting his bared head and the wind blowing astray his abundant youthful hair. The uncovered head became synonymous with the "bald eagle." It was, and is to this day, the image of American manhood.

In addition, Americans seek simplicity. They denigrate all cumbersome modes of attire and patterns that exacerbate their freedom of movement. The greatest problem of a hat—the one rarely discussed but crucial to the issue—is, what's to be done with it indoors? If worn (on one's head, of course), it is viewed by certain purveyors of "good taste" as a breach of etiquette. Never will I forget my attempt as a youth to visit the bastion of American Judaism on Fifth Avenue in New York City. I simply wished to personally observe this unique Reform citadel.

Having barely crossed the portals of the front door I was accosted by a belligerent, scolding shout: "Young man. Have you no respect?" Being young and naive, as well as completely innocent of any wrongdoing, I couldn't imagine any conscious or even indirect misconduct. Shortly I was informed of my sin of omission. I had been guilty of wearing an outdoor hat inside the "holy temple." What a crime! Being a young yeshivah student accustomed to wearing a hat certainly in a synagogue, the culture shock was so great that I immediately departed. In fact, I still remember considering the affront as an act of divine retribution for attempting to satisfy a bizarre curiosity.

So wearing a hat indoors, in certain circles, is certainly not the means of winning friends and gaining a reputation for sophistication.

To place the hat on an adjacent vacant chair is also not a remedy. Sooner or later someone will squash your hat by sitting on it; or even worse, publicly request the owner of the hat to please remove it.

To put your hat on the table, to some, is even worse than wearing it indoors. Also, your area is marked as the place with the hat. And, of course, to carry it is just an awkward scene.

Perhaps to eliminate this traumatic problem people decided that it just wasn't worth it to wear a hat at all. Not having a hat thus frees the movement of a man. Isn't that what democracy is all about?

Also, if one doesn't wear a hat one may not even have to wear a tie. Thus, informality is but another ancillary benefit of eliminating a hat.

Yet I still wear a hat. In fact, all of the above reasons have no impact upon my habit at all. Why?

I wear a hat because it has been ingrained within me that a religious Jew covers his head. It's my pride of culture and my badge of belief. It's the mainstream of Judaism.

The Talmud (*Kiddushin* 31a) notes that "Rav Huna, son of Rav Yehoshua, would not walk four cubits bareheaded, saying, 'The Divine Presence is above my head.' " Thus, the covering of one's head is a formal symbolic manifestation of the constant presence of God. As the psalmist states (23:4): "Yea, though I walk through the valley of the shadow of death, I shall fear no evil, for Thou art with me." My God is always above me. I am covered by the protection of my God. My hat is a constant reminder that the Jew is never alone. He walks with God. It is a feeling of assurance and comfort. At the same time an ever-present conscience to withhold one from going astray.

But my head covering has another role. It is a symbol of humility. How enlightening it is that the Talmud presents the concept of covering one's head directly adjacent to a statement prohibiting one from "walking with the haughty."

The most distinct human quality of man is his mind. It's his essence. Yet it must be controlled. It is constantly covered as a shield against arrogance. The greatest treasure of man—his mind—is always withheld from public scrutiny; hidden like a priceless heirloom; controlled by the presence of God. Yes, the bareheaded man is a symbol of pride and, perhaps, arrogance. His head is in the clouds. Not so the Jew. His head is covered to remind him of his limits, frailties and ever-dependence upon God. The hat, or yarmulke, is the daily implementation of the rule in Proverbs (1:7) that "the fear of the Lord is the beginning of knowledge." It is the intertwining of religion and wisdom.

Since the presence of God permeates our existence (and is not only experienced in the synagogue), tradition has been to cover the head throughout all pursuits of life: in and out of the synagogue and home.

In talmudic times, moreover, the type of hat worn was a visible means of determining status. A married man wore a different covering than a single person (*Kiddushin* 29b). A scholar, moreover, had a distinctive hat (ibid. 8a—Rav Ka-hanna, also 30a—R. Yeshoshua b. Levi; see Rashi). Even today, the type of hat worn marks a distinctive brand of Jewish ritual practice. The Polish Chassidic high fur hat is radically distinct from the flat Hungarian style (shtreimel). The curve of the hat brim and the height of the crown immediately reveal the dialect and ancestry of a Chassidic Jew. The rabbi's homburg marks his presence as readily as his Torah. A means of delineating modern-day yeshivot from the deeply frum (religious) institu-tions is to classify the latter as the "black hats." Indeed, the knitted yarmulke (kipa s'ruga) portrays a message as potent as the black hat. It manifests that the person loves Israel, is modern, and yet openly wishes to display his Jewish identity to all. Some, just the opposite, do not wish to so overtly show their Jewishness. They have been ingrained by generations of fear to not wear a yarmulke in the streets. Others contend that a hat rather than a yarmulke is a more formal means of attire. Each style is symptomatic of a distinct religious orientation to life. In addition, the mystics maintain that the greater the involvement with kedushah (sanctity), the more should one's material body be covered. Many, therefore, will wear hats on Shabbat to signify the added sanctity of the day; their Shabbat hats are, moreover, different from those worn throughout the week. Indeed, to some, wearing a hat indoors is certainly not a breach of etiquette but, just the opposite, a mark of great respect and reverence.

The Talmud notes that the placing of a covering on one's head is as natural to the Jew as rising in the morning and getting dressed with clothes. In Berachot (60b) the Talmud contends that each process of awakening has a concomitant blessing. For example: "When he opens his eyes, he should say: 'Blessed is He who opens the eyes of the blind.' . . . When he dresses he should say, 'Blessed is he who clothes the naked.' . . . When he places a covering on his head, he should say, 'Blessed is He who crowns Israel with glory.' "

In other words the covering of one's head is part of the

process of getting dressed in the morning. It's inconceivable that the Jew would not place a covering on his head.

Indeed, the significance of the blessing relates to the primary religious role of the hat (or yarmulke).

The Jew makes numerous *berachot* (blessings) throughout the day. Prior to the performance of any mitzvah, the Jew acknowledges its sanctity by chanting a blessing. Why is it that the all-pervasive mitzvah of believing in God has no *berachah* each day? A partial response is that blessings were instituted as preparatory statements prior to specific actions. Blessings were never set up for the obligations of the heart or the mind. Yet by placing a covering on one's head each day one is concretely and actively manifesting the presence of God. Thus the blessing of covering one's head is, in reality, the *berachah* of belief. For God is the glory of the Jew.

Is it no wonder that my head is always covered? A Jew covers his head. Some by means of a hat; others by their yarmulke. Each to his own brand of Judaism. Whatever the style, a Jew covers his head. It is his tag of identification; it overtly stamps him as a believing Jew. It is the essence of belief.

37. *An Analysis of Torah Study*

On Sinai the Jewish people proudly received the Torah and firmly proclaimed both their acceptance of its lofty ideals and their dedication to its sacred laws by saying, "All that the Lord has spoken *na'aseh ve'nishmah*—we will do and we will seek to understand" (Exodus 24:7).

This profound biblical statement of faith has historically and traditionally been revered as an articulate formulation of the essence of Torah and the unique orientation required of its adherents.

One of the primary reasons why this verse is considered so important is due to a unique observation found in the ancient kabbalistic work, the *Zohar*. The *Zohar* says that while *na'aseh* refers to a commitment to do good deeds and to observe mitzvot, *ve'nishmah* relates to an involvement in the study of Torah. Thus, the Jews on Sinai made a dual commitment. While on one hand, they asserted their readiness to observe God's commandments, on the other they made a distinct affirmation of their willingness to study Torah.

This dichotomy, this necessity to clearly construct a line of demarcation between the observance of commandments and the study of Torah, is directly related to the twofold aim of Torah education itself.

The pursuit of Torah knowledge is a means to better observe commandments as well as an end in itself.

To be a good Jew, to carefully and scrupulously follow the dictates of our religion, it is necessary to be well acquainted with many of its laws and customs. Indeed, it is written that an ignoramus cannot be a pious person. This is quite understandable, for one who is ignorant of Judaism certainly cannot know when he is doing something right or wrong. It is, moreover, practically impossible to observe the Shabbat if one is ignorant of the intricate, detailed laws of this holy day. Thus, Torah study serves as the vehicle to stimulate the observance of mitzvot.

Yet there is another important facet to the study of Torah. This is the obligation to study Torah for its own sake. This portion of education is not a means to observe commandments but, rather, a mitzvah in itself. Just as kashrut and putting on of tefillin are commandments, so too is the study of Torah. This obligation is also incumbent upon one who considers himself a grand master in all aspects of the law. Even he who feels he knows the entire Torah is still obligated to learn. The Talmud portrays this concept when it relates that a tanna asked whether he who was well versed in all aspects of the Torah was free from the obligation to study it. The answer presented was that if one should find a period of time which was neither a part of the day nor a portion of the night, only then would he be absolved of all requirements to learn Torah (*Menachot* 99*b*).

It is interesting to note that there is a great practical distinction between the two approaches to the study of Torah. Should Torah study be simply a means of enabling one to acquire the technical knowledge necessary for an observant Jew, then one could, perhaps, free himself from any obligation to learn by availing himself of the services of a scholar who would outline all needed for observance. To the extent that men must study Torah for its own sake, no such situation or excuse would be valid. Just as the rabbi's act of putting on tefillin or observing the Shabbat does not in any way free others from these mitzvot, so too does the rabbi's intense scholarship affect in no way the requirement of all to spend a portion of time learning Torah.

Learning Torah for its own sake may be compared to the study of pure science. In the latter, one seeks knowledge of the intracacies of the world of existence, without actual care to its productive modern application. In the former, one seeks comprehension of the wisdom of the Almighty, without regard to whether the knowledge gained is functional or applicable to modern life. The Torah is the revealed word of God to man. Studying the Torah is, therefore, the highest act of religious piety, for it is an endeavor to comprehend the divine will.

Thus, according to the *Zohar*, this is the meaning of the dual commitment of *na'aseh ve'nishmah*. *Na'aseh*, we will do mitzvot and we will learn all the necessary laws for their observance. Yet *ve'nishmah*, we will also dedicate ourselves to the study of Torah for its own sake. This unique formulation of Torah is the key to the behavioral pattern of countless Jews in all spheres of life, rich or poor, wise or ignorant, rabbi or layman, professional or businessman, who intensely study Torah in all spare moments available. This too is the key to why some spend a lifetime devoted to Torah study. Even those who are busy, even those overloaded with obligations, are required to make time for the observance of such a pure and refined mitzvah, the study of Torah itself.

38. The Rabbi and the Synagogue

The formal installation of a new rabbi is not a mere festive occasion of a synagogue. It is, rather, the celebration of the creation of a unique charismatic entity; a new symbiotic convergence of religious forces which grants to both rabbi and synagogue an enlarged capacity for leadership that surpasses the potential of each individual component.

The synagogue has served a vital function in the history of Jewish survival. When the ancient Holy Temple was scorched to the ground, Jerusalem destroyed, and the Jewish people dispersed throughout the world, a spirit of Jewish pride continued to prevail in the diaspora. From the ashes of the ancient Holy Temple, Jews established, through the far-flung bastions of civilization, vehicles to sustain their identity.

Wherever the Jew traveled, he replicated the Holy Temple by creating synagogues. From Babylonia to North Africa, from Spain to Europe, from America to the Third World, the synagogue was formed as the symbolic mark of Jewish residence and the prime vehicle for the transmission of Jewish culture.

Indeed, the synagogue became one of the most popular of all Jewish traditions and rituals and served as the rallying force to attract Jews of all persuasions and all levels of observance. It became the central address for Jewish communal life throughout the world.

At the same time, the synagogue became the first institution that our enemies sought to destroy. From the scriptural Balaam till Kristallnacht, to the communists in our day, the synagogue has always been the first victim in any onslaught to destroy Jewish values and Jewish identity.

In Hebrew the synagogue is called *bait haknesset*, which means the "house of assemblage," or "gathering." Even though the primary function of a synagogue is to serve as a house of prayer, nowhere is the function of prayer in any way involved in its traditional name. This suggests a clue to the true function and role of the synagogue. There is a tradition that the name given to an entity in some way defines its essential quality. Thus the term *bait haknesset* tells us what the synagogue is all about. Formed in the diaspora, it is really not a pure replica of the ancient Temple, for it possesses unique diaspora features. It has functions that replicate the new status of the people and the climate of Torah. The name *bait haknesset* teaches us that the role of the Jew is to gather together with his fellow Jews within the framework of religious devotion. This implies the following key concerns.

1. The Jew in diaspora may be alone, spatially separated from his homeland, but he is not lonely. He gathers together with his people in a sanctuary. He bonds himself with a prayer of love for Israel and support for *Medinat Yisrael*. No matter the concern of the Jewish people, whether political, communal, charitable, educational, or devotional, there must be one central gathering area, and that place must be associated with prayer. The priorities of the Jew are religious in nature and must be resolved in a holy place.

2. The synagogue is not the Holy Temple. The Holy Temple was the one central spatial citadel of Jewish concern. As Jews spread throughout the world they recognized that religion was not rooted in space but in time. Diaspora did not imply the end of the Jewish people or the dissolution of our Torah. Synagogues may be formed; houses of worship may be created in the far-flung corners of the world. The goal of the Jew was not to conquer space but to sanctify time. At the same periods of time each year, Jews would gather in their synagogues

throughout the world and pray to the same God. The synagogue was, therefore, a reaffirmation of the timeless eternity of our people and the continuity of our tradition.

3. The synagogue also was the democratization of Jewish devotion. In the past, priests *(kohanim)* served as the agents of the people for devotional purposes. The institution of the synagogue democratized prayer. No agents were necessary for the Jew to pray. No third parties served as vehicles for the service of God. Each man prayed together with his fellow Jews directly to the Almighty. The synagogues, therefore, were gathering houses for the Jew to express his communal feelings, empathy, and relationship to the Almighty. It was not a Temple, a sanctuary based upon holy ground requiring holy instruments and holy people. It made every Jew an agent of God and every land a proper citadel.

4. Maimonides maintains that in ancient times when the leader of the Sanhedrin was selected, his role was to serve "in the place of Moses." The meaning is that every lawgiver must have roots to Mount Sinai. Moses was the first lawgiver. Every leader in every community must address his roots and base his inspiration upon the tradition of Sinai. The synagogue may be rooted in time and not space. The synagogue may be the gathering place of Jews for all matters of Jewish communal interest. It may be the democratization of religious devotion, but it is not a place of *hefker*. It is not rootless. It is not built upon a vacuum. Its rabbi, its spiritual leader, gives guidance to it on the principles expounded from generation to generation, from father to son, from master to disciple, from the Almighty to Moses? This imposes upon the rabbi an awesome obligation to recreate, together with the congregation, the climate of Sinai. Therein the people stated, as recorded in the Scripture, that Moses was the lawgiver and that the people requested that he impart to them the Torah learned from God. No rabbi is comparable to Moses. No rabbi in our day and age has direct channels to God, but he must replicate in any way possible the traditions of Sinai and the charismatic leadership of *Mesora*.

The Torah tells us that the Jews rested by Mount Sinai (Exodus 19:2), and Rashi relates that the singular term used *(vayichan)* tells us that the people were together as if they were one body and one heart. There was harmony. There was unity of purpose, friendship, and comradery. This is the goal in addition to the teaching of Torah—to recreate the unity of Sinai. The word *vayichan* is derived from the word *chayn*, which means "charm, grace." When there is charm, when there is grace, when there is kindness, there is respect, there is finesse, there is unity between one and another. This then is the task of the rabbi and the synagogue. This relationship, once started, should, with the blessing of the Almighty, continue to go on to the never-ending tomorrows of the future.

Robert Browning, the famous poet, in his poem entitled "Rabbi Ben Ezra," once said, "Grow old along with me!/The best is yet to be,/The last of life, for which the first was made." This is our prayer for the Jewish community. "Grow old along with me, the best is yet to be." Amen.

II. Holiday Concerns

39. Why Pray in a Synagogue on the High Holidays?

Rosh Hashanah is a time for contemplation, a moment to rethink the merits of our past. Major decisions are to be made. "Who will live, who will die? Who will be healthy? Who will live, yet with an agonizing sigh!"

It deals with the most personalized, private concern of any person. I know not of any man or woman who would not give up the mad rush for materialism or the veneer of luxury when faced with the imminent choice of life over death.

And yet, somehow, this crucial, private dilemma is simply not stressed in our prayers at all. Nowhere do we talk or pray about our personal problems. Nowhere is any mention made about me, my issues, or my private problems. Every single prayer on this holiday is written in the plural construct.

We say; "Our Father, Our King, we have sinned before You." Why must I mention the sins of others? I and you should only be concerned with our own crimes, our own conscious and unwitting errors. Why must I assume automatically that others have also sinned? Does it lessen my faults? By detailing the sins of others I have no time to concentrate upon my own problems.

Even our aspirations are diluted with communal sensations. "Remember us for life, O King who desires life, and inscribe us in the Book of Life." Is this prayer realistic? Or deep down, in

107

the far reaches of our souls, are we really concerned primarily with numero uno—me, you, ourselves? And yet no prayer addresses the personalized, private wishes of our hearts.

Indeed, there is one exception to the rule. It is the prayer chanted by the *chazzan* prior to *Musaf:* the *Heinneni.* In it the cantor is making a private appeal to God. The prayer is in the singular form. He notes his unworthiness to represent the people and prays that he be considered comparable to one who is replete with piety and righteousness. But you or I have no such prayer. Why not?

Many years ago while a college student, I had an interview with a prominent professor of philosophy. As I entered her office, the lights were out, the room was completely dark, soft symphonic music echoed in the background, and lying on a couch with closed eyes, immobile, was this old woman apparently asleep. I didn't know what to do. I even thought that maybe she was dead. Yet somehow my presence was felt; she awoke, went to her desk, welcomed me, and conducted a thorough, rational discussion with me about a philosophical issue. But my mind was on the scene I had witnessed. So I asked her about it. I mentioned that it appeared somewhat bizarre and strange. With laughter in her voice, she noted the following. "I am paid to think," she said. "As a result, I don't think in a haphazard fashion. I work at it. I set up hours each day just to think through problems. The darkness and the music are to set the mood to stimulate thoughts and mitigate distractions."

This incident made a traumatic impact upon me. She was right. Thinking is the most human of our functions. There's no shame in thinking through issues. So each day I set aside time to think and to learn. I don't close my eyes, darken the room, or require music. But I need privacy. I like it quiet. I sit by myself and mentally discuss the pros and cons of issues. I attempt to rationally explore a problem to its logical conclusion, or to note that I simply cannot resolve the issue.

Whatever the case, serious thought mandates concentration. We all need it. Yet we scoff at it. We like activity, action, movement. If a person does not display activity, we denigrate the process of contemplation. A philosoff! Yet we all manifest this process in one form or another.

As a result, the davening in a shul on a Day of Judgment seems somewhat contrary to the essence of contemplation. Hardly anyone who seeks to understand himself or herself likes crowds. How can I think about me today in a congregation of such a size? Some are talking, some praying, others singing, still others crying. Is this the place to think? I'm in court. My life is to be decided. Should I not be alone! Alone with my private feelings. Alone with my loved ones. Look at your neighbors in the synagogue. Is our fate so intertwined with them that not only must I pray for them as well as me, but I have to sit with them too? Why does the Machzor and the aura of the High Holidays so totally disregard these feelings?

Perhaps the questions posed draw attention to the real message of Rosh Hashanah and its essential goals, values somehow forgotten or neglected to be learned or taught.

I think a story, a true story, will best articulate the issue. It is known that Dr. Nachum Goldmann went on aliyah to Israel and settled in Jerusalem. This man was one of the foremost communal leaders of our people. He was the leader of the World Zionist Organization. He was active in almost all major issues affecting Jews in the diaspora as well as Israel. He was controversial, both loved and hated, familiar to most of the leading political personalities of our age. As a result, his aliyah to Israel was considered a coup. The fact that this prominent secular Jew could leave the golden *galut* and settle in Israel was considered an omen that aliyah was a realistic probability for the Western Jew. As a result, his coming to Israel was featured in all the papers and heralded as a victory for Israel and Zionism.

Shortly after his arrival, his home was robbed. To the extent that his presence created such an interest, the robbery also was front-page news. The concern was that this robbery against such a distinguished immigrant would cast negative ramifications on the entire aliyah movement. Why escape the *galut?* Why leave America, so the argument ran, if you can be robbed in Jerusalem? If a Jew is not safe in Jerusalem, then why come there at all? Look at what happened to Dr. Goldmann.

Thus, the robbery became an international incident flashed throughout the world media.

Because of such notoriety, the chief of police of Jerusalem set up a special investigative team to apprehend the criminals. After some time the police were fortunate. They captured and jailed the robbers. Dr. Goldmann was informed of this and requested the opportunity to personally meet with them. The request was granted, and Dr. Goldmann went to speak with them. He looked at them for some time and then said, "I want you to know that I don't forgive you. I don't forgive you at all!"

One of the criminals looked at him in amazement. "Who are you not to forgive? Your property has been returned. You haven't lost anything, all you had was a period of inconvenience. Why are you so supermoral? Do you think you're so special because you're so rich and prominent? We've been caught. Now we'll have to pay for our crimes. We'll be punished. How dare you talk of not forgiving us? You know not our problems. A Jew forgives another Jew. Don't be so high and moral. Don't put your problems on our conscience."

After this outburst, Dr. Goldmann said: "You don't understand. It's not the crime against me that I'm concerned with. Your robbery of my personal possessions is of no importance. Your crime against me I forgive you. But I cannot forgive you for the greater crime that you committed." He pointed his finger at them and in a quavering voice, said, "You sinned against Israel." He raised his voice and repeated, "You sinned against Israel and Jerusalem. You made a bad mark upon Jerusalem. You denigrated the *kavod* of our holy city. You made aliyah into a farce. I have not the power to condone such a crime."

Hearing this outburst, the prisoner screamed out. "Not so! I fought in the war to save Israel. Never would I hurt my nation. It's you I sinned against."

"No," said Dr. Goldmann. "That's what you thought you did. But that's not what happened. You sinned against Israel. You made Israel suffer." And he walked out.

The story concludes with a letter that Dr. Goldmann received several years after the incident. The letter was from the prisoners. It stated that Dr. Goldmann's words had so impacted their souls that they truly felt remorse and had decided to make amends by studying to be social workers helping the poor and needy of their people. This, they felt, would atone for their grievous crime against the people, the nation, and the city they loved.

This story suggests the key to the understanding of Rosh Hashanah.

Rosh Hashanah is the Day of Judgment. Yet a close reading of our sacred literature reveals that it is not the *only* Day of Judgment. The Mishnah (Rosh Hashanah 16a) says that the world is judged at four different periods of time. On Pesach for grain, and on Shavuot for fruit. On Sukkot for water, and on Rosh Hashanah we pass like sheep before our Master. Wherein lies the distinction between the judgment of Rosh Hashanah versus the other periods of time? Rabbi Yossi said: "Man is judged daily." Rabbi Nathan went further: "Man is judged every hour." And so indeed we may be. If so, what is the judgment of Rosh Hashanah?

I suggest the following. Perhaps a key element of Rosh Hashanah is the consideration of the sins we have committed against our people, our nation, our community, and our holy city, Yerushalayim.

We stand in scrutiny for lifting the banner of Israel or for denigrating the *kavod* of our people.

Every act of man has a social component attached to it. No man is a hermit. No person lives in his or her own island. No person can be a *tzaddik* in peltz, which suggests that if he is warm and fine, he may disregard the needs of others.

Every sin I may have committed, every immoral or irreligious act, has ramifications upon the status of religion, the posture of Jewish communal life, and the *kavod* of our people.

No one can, therefore, pray alone in private. For Rosh Hashanah assesses the communal guilts we have made. Look at our people. Sit next to them. Hear them. Be a physical part of their lives. And then explore, *explore* your soul—and assess whether you let them down or not this past year. Our private concerns—yes, at home we can analyze them quite well. But never, never can our responsibilities to others be known shielded from the physical impact of a synagogue.

For this reason, our prayers are in the plural. For each person has to feel that he alone, or she alone, has lifted up the *kavod* of our people or brought it down. "Who will live or die" refers not only to me or you. It now has an expanded format. Who will live or who will die because of me? Who will prosper because of my actions? Who will suffer because of me? The Vilna Gaon, in his commentary to the fifth chapter of *Berachot*, even suggests that any prayer written in the plural form should not be chanted with personal intentions. It is written for the community, and communal thoughts should permeate the process. Any person who wishes to personalize the prayers should add his own words and sentiments.

My friends, this is what coming to shul to pray is all about. This is what synagogue life is all about. And even more, this is what Rosh Hashanah is all about. Let us pray well. But at least we know now what we are doing.

40. The Synagogue and the Akedah

Rosh Hashanah has a mood of its own. It celebrates the creation of the world: mankind's beginning and a time for pensive recollections. All over the world Jews gather together in synagogues to share common prayers and to express bonds of mutual Jewish identity and friendship. It is the synagogue that is the physical catalyst to bond us together. It, therefore, is most appropriate to discuss on Rosh Hashanah the spiritual origins and symbolic messages of the roots of synagogue life.

To guide our thoughts, it is necessary to analyze a story of the past: a story read in the Torah on Rosh Hashanah, with profound meanings for all time. The Torah tells us that the Almighty commanded Abraham to take his son Isaac, the son he so truly loved, the child he had waited so many years to have—to take this son and to offer him as a sacrifice to God. Without a murmur of dissent, Abraham proceeded to carry out the divine command. Together with Isaac, he ascended the holy mountain and prepared his son for the sacrifice. Just as he was about to commit the awesome act a heavenly voice said: "Do not touch your child, do not harm him; you have shown your commitment. Behold, there is a ram whose horns are caught in the thicket. Sacrifice the ram, not your son." (Gen. 22)

The Midrash relates that at that time a heavenly decision was made to designate the site as the place of the Holy Temple—for sacred prayer.

Why? What special significance did the site and the sacrifice

113

have for prayer? What unique message did the sacrifice manifest for future generations?

Let us review the biblical story. Picture in your minds the awesome decree. What did Abraham do? Did he question God? Did he hesitate or refuse? No. He was such a believer—so strong was his commitment—that no sacrifice was too great. An ordinary man would definitely have balked. Should not Abraham have said, "Enough—how much can be expected or demanded of one man? My whole life has been devoted to others. Why should I always be selected for tests? Why not others? Why not those who never consider and never respond to the needs of their fellow man? Why not them? Why my child?" But Abraham displayed perfect composure. A truly dedicated person looks not upon others. It does not disturb him how much or how little others have done or given. If he believes in his goal; if he sees the importance, recognizes the need—he cares not what he has already done in the past, but rather, whether he can yet do more. Abraham believed that he could always do more. This was Abraham. What about Isaac? Isaac was not a child but a grown man in his thirties. The Midrash informs us that he knew, he knew well, his father's awesome plans. Yet he calmly submitted himself to sacrifice his own life. Is this not unique? Why did Yitzchok do it? He was not commanded by God. His father was—not he. He should have rebelled. He had no vision. God never commanded him to sacrifice his life. The only way that Isaac knew of the matter was through the words and actions of his father. This, then, is Isaac's lesson to humanity: that what a father says is similar to the command of God. A father does not lie; his word is holy. That such a wonderfully intense relationship was established between a father and a son—such love, such unity, that a son was willing to sacrifice his own life, if that was his father's will. At the moment of truth, when Isaac thought he would die, the Midrash tells us that he said, *ma a'aseh l'dami*, which is interpreted to mean, "What will I do about my mother?" How will she be able to bear the loss of her son? Isaac was willing to give up his life, but his last concern was for his mother. How will she feel? He was not concerned with his life but his mother's composure. His mother would have to live knowing her son was gone. This bothered him. This was his primary concern.

For these reasons the Almighty designated the site as a holy citadel for prayer. A place with memories of unselfish sacrifice and total dedication; of family love; of a child willing to do all— even give up his life out of respect for the honor of his father; a place wherein there is a concern for the future; for the agony and suffering of others.

Is this not the apex of human grandeur? Is this not a proper sanctuary for prayer? But the site was not formally hallowed and proclaimed until another incident occurred. An incident that transpired with Jacob, Abraham's grandson. Scripture informs us that Jacob fled the jealous animosity of his twin brother Esau. Fleeing, he passed over a certain place and had a unique sensation. He felt that he had recently passed over the site, hallowed by the prayers of his father and grandfather, Abraham and Isaac. The Midrash tells us that at first he did not want to return. He wanted yet to flee. He was in a desert— haggard, tired, running away from the murderous intentions of his brother. For fourteen years he was away from his father's home, from his father's rituals, his father's prayers. He was both spatially and emotionally on his own. But the Midrash tells us: "Is it possible that I can pass over a place where my parents prayed and I did not pray?" He felt roots. He felt a family tie. No matter what the danger, he had to return. No matter how far he was from his family, he had to return. His father davened there; his grandfather davened there; that's where he should daven too. That's where he belonged. He returned.

Esau wants to kill Jacob, and Jacob builds a shul. He returned and prayed and saw a vision of a ladder going up till the heaven; a vision depicting the grandeur, the heights to which man can aspire. He felt relaxed, he felt pride; he felt good inside, he built an altar and said: "This is the house of God. This is the gateway to heaven." It is not enough to designate a place to be a house of worship. Man must appreciate it; man must lend a hand; man must support it. Man must say: "This is the house of God. Here are my roots. Here is where my people are; this is my spiritual home."

This is what Rosh Hashanah is all about. This is why we pray in a synagogue.

41. A Child's Prayer

Rosh Hashanah is a most unique and glorious period of time. Indeed, it creates and possesses a mood so vastly different from all we know and all we experience throughout the year. Somehow, the searching strands of the holiday service pierce the reserve and shatter the indifference built up in our hearts toward matters called divine. At this time, in these precious moments, our thoughts, our emotions are closer to God, closer to religious convictions, and nearer to positive Jewish values than at any other period in the long-drawn-out, activity-packed days of the yearly cycle.

On such an occasion we must direct our attention to the decisive and realistic questions of the day. Namely, can we change? Do we have a chance? Can we who have lived an entire year with an estranged heart and deaf ear to so many Jewish laws, values, and traditions expect God to listen to our prayers? And most important of all, how can we best utilize this solemn moment?

To guide our thoughts and partially answer these vital questions, I believe it necessary to analyze a story of the past. A story written in the past but with profound meaning for all times. A story of a family dilemma and a child's prayer.

The Bible weaves a penetrating tale of Abraham's dedication and piety. It tells how he traveled from place to place teaching all the sublime belief in One God, the importance of hospitality, and the need for moral and ethical patterns of behavior. But was this man happy? Was Abraham content with his life? No, not at all.

117

He wanted a son, a son whom he could teach. A son who would continue to spread the word of God after he was gone. His wife, his lovely, beautiful wife for so many, many years, was sterile. She couldn't have any children at all. Sarah, she too wanted a child; she too saw the anguish of her husband Abraham. And one day, because of her love, because of her complete devotion to Abraham, she did something that people today would recognize as an unbelievably great sacrifice for love. Sarah, knowing her painful inability to have a child, forcefully persuaded Abraham to marry her own maid and servant, Hagar, in order to have a child.

Now, this happened in a time when it was the common practice for a man to have more than one wife. There were no rules as today condemning such matters. But rules or no rules, practices or no practices, there are feelings, emotions strong and vibrant, that negate such actions. Indeed, even in those days for a woman to initiate such action, to encourage and convince her husband of the correctness of such a procedure and to take her own slave and maid-servant and make her an equal, was certainly an unbelievable sacrifice for love.

Abraham married Hagar, and shortly she became pregnant and gave birth to a son called Ishmael. Did Hagar repay Sarah's kindness? She repaid Sarah, but not with kindness. Hagar now found herself in a very firm and secure position. She not only felt equal to Sarah, but quite superior. Hagar had a child, a son from Abraham, and in every cruel and mean way she brought home this fact to Sarah. When they were together, Hagar would speak of how wonderful it was to have a child; how much more a husband loves a wife who is the mother of his son. The plight of Sarah was most tragic and unfortunate. Then one day, when Sarah was getting on in her years, when her hope for a son had almost waned, God answered her prayers and she gave birth to Isaac. It is now that the real drama begins to unfold.

Sarah recognized that having a child at her age was a miraculous event. A child given her when hope had almost faded was destined for greatness. She, therefore, began to watch him very carefully and to supervise his activities. What she saw, she did not like. She noted her son playing with Ishmael and began to investigate the type of a friend her child had. She overheard Ishmael telling his other friends that Abraham was not the true father of Isaac and that he, he alone, was the sole heir of Abraham. These remarks were most disturbing to Sarah. Besides the personal shame and hurt that she felt, Sarah began to worry about her son. Was this the type of a friend that Isaac should have? This is not a proper friend. Sarah then began to notice that Ishmael was also a *m'tzachayk*, a person who laughed at the vile crime of murder, a boy who viewed the seriousness of adultery with mockery; a child who worshipped idols and scoffed at its evil ramifications. No, no, this could not be. This was no environment for her child.

Her child hadn't a chance if he was a friend of Ishmael. How could he grow? How could he learn the beauties of life if his friend mocked the most serious of crimes? How could a little child absorb proper values if his best friend had none? How could a boy learn correct values if his friend negated all that is good?

Sarah made a decision. Ishmael must leave before little Isaac's mind was contaminated. But not only Ishmael, Hagar the mother, she too must leave Abraham's household. Indeed, she must be the cause of Ishmael's corrupt, valueless mind. How else? Where in such a pious household of Abraham could he have acquired such debased traits? When a child has no values one looks to the parents for the cause, and it certainly couldn't be the holy Abraham. Hagar, the ungrateful, she must be the seed of all this corruption. Sarah went to Abraham, told him her tale, and demanded that the moral and religious future of their child necessitated the banishment of Ishmael and

Hagar. She let him know that unless this drastic measure was taken, Ishmael and Hagar would corrode Isaac's inherent goodness.

Abraham was troubled and knew not what to do. Could he or should he banish part of his own family? To guide his actions Abraham sought counsel from his Heavenly Father. God said, "All that Sarah tells you, listen to her." Listen to your wife, she knows what she is saying. She is with the young children so much more than you. What she has heard, what she has seen is true, Isaac will follow in your ways, but not if he learns from the corrupter, Ishmael. Send Ishmael and Hagar away. Hearkening to the divine command, the wishes of his wife, and the desire for moral family living, Hagar and Ishmael were sent away.

Seeking safety, the mother and child lost their way and unwittingly found themselves in the complex maze of a vast, seemingly endless, parched desert. Seeing no hope, no route to escape, Hagar went aside, left Ishmael alone, and began to weep and bemoan her plight. Ishmael at that time felt more alone and lonely than at any other moment in his entire life. He looked around—saw the empty, vast, hot, dry sands of the endless desert, heard the moaning sobs of his crying mother, and all his mocking, hardened, debased negative feelings towards God shriveled into quakes of fear. Ishmael began to cry and call out to God for help. The Bible says that God heard the cries of the youth and saved him, *b'asher hu sham*—"because of where he was" (Gen. 21:17). Picture this! A person who laughs at the crime of murder, sees nothing wrong with adultery, is saved by God. A boy who is later to become the leader of the Arab nation—an actual thief, murderer, and pillager of nations. A boy whose past is evil and whose future is heinous. A son of an ungrateful mother, who disrespects his father, and corrupts youth. Such a person cries to God, and wonder of wonders, his prayers are answered. God saves him.

This is the final episode in our dramatic portrayal. An insight into the intricate nature of prayer itself. We see, from all we've heard, that for divine help, not an absolute purity of soul or salvation but divine help and providence, God looks not at the past, no matter how terrible it is, nor at the future, no matter how dark it appears, but *b'asher hu sham*, at the present, where you are now. What you are presently thinking, doing, and feeling. No matter what you have been or whatever you shall be, if now, right now, you are sincere, full of conviction and genuinely sorry for past errors and resolve to change the future, you deserve a chance. A chance to make it. Whether you do or do not, that is not the present concern.

What chance do we have? Will God listen to our prayers? The answer has already been presented. All the opportunities in the world are before us. All we have to do is try. If God will listen to the prayers of Ishmael, he will certainly hearken to ours. We will be judged and saved by the sincerity of today. We stand alone, not lonely but alone, before our Creator. It is our moment of destiny. Today is the Day of Judgment, and it is for today's actions that we will be judged. Now is the time to bring our own salvation. Let us not waste our last chance to return.

42. Adam's Sin

Rosh Hashanah commemorates the creation of the world. Tradition has it that it is also the day when Adam, the first man, was judged for committing the first sin. Each year we acknowledge that event by being judged for our sins. Accordingly, by understanding Adam's sin we may derive some meaning of the process of heavenly judgment.

Adam, formed by God, was placed in the Garden of Eden. Subsequently, Eve was created to be his helpmate. Both were granted freedom to partake of all pleasures. They had only one negative command: a prohibition of eating from the tree of knowledge. This command was violated, and Adam and Eve were banished from the Garden of Eden.

What was the severity of their sin? Do we not all violate commands? Why was their punishment so traumatically oppressive?

A brief understanding of Scripture may provide insight into the issue. In the story of creation, the Bible notes, "And no herb of the field had yet grown: for the Lord God had not caused it to rain upon the earth, and there was not a man to till the ground" (Genesis 2:5).

Commenting upon this verse, Rashi makes a most unusual statement. He suggests that the reason why God did not cause rain to fall was simply because man, Adam, had not been created yet to work it and appreciate the blessings of rain. The Maharal of Prague elaborates upon this issue by saying that the Bible teaches us a fundamental law of nature. A gift must be appreciated. Indeed, appreciation—*hakarat hatov* (recognition of the good that others do for us)—is the glue that cements relationships; without it, all communal and social dynamics fall apart.

Let us now review our story of Adam. How does Adam respond to God? He says, "The woman whom Thou gave me—she gave me of the forbidden fruit to eat." (Gen. 3:12). In other words, I didn't ask for a wife. God gave her to me. It was Your idea. You suggested I need her. It was Your gift which perverted my morality.

This was the key traumatic element of Adam's sin. He was an ingrate. He renounced and repudiated the merit of his gift. Instead of being appreciative, he was scornful.

How many today appreciate what others do for them? Instead of thanking them for their efforts, we blame them, their gifts, and their service for our faults. Instead of thanking our spouses and friends for all they've done for us we castigate them for our errors.

The lack of ability to thank God for our goodness cries out as a key sin of our lives.

Instead of *Baruch Hashem*—"Thank God," we bemoan our plight.

This concept was not lost on a previous generation. "How are you?" one would ask. *"Baruch Hashem*—thank God" was the answer.

"How is your wife? your children? your job? life itself?" *"Baruch Hashem*—thank God" was the answer. Such responses were not construed, as they are today as acts of excessive piety. They were not merely affirmations of faith, but, rather, words of appreciation. They recognized the gift of life itself. They thanked God for the ability to live, love, and enjoy life—facts we mostly recognize only when we are sick.

So, as we part from the High Holiday services, let us not commit Adam's sin again. Let us not institutionalize his errors.

At the same time, let us make *Baruch Hashem,* not an empty, hackneyed cliché, but an echo of our character. We are people who appreciate the goodness done to us. And at the time when we study our faults, we can feel the love given us by God and man.

To appreciate means to respond. To respond means to give. And to get in return. That is what life is all about.

43. Rosh Hashanah: To Love Others

Rosh Hashanah is here again. Once again it is time to reflect upon our lifestyle and to pass personal judgment upon our actions. We don't request our friends to judge us. We do not want our neighbors to assess our character. This is a role we assume for ourselves. It is a difficult, arduous process to judge oneself. It is much easier to evaluate others. It is so much more convenient to direct friends to alter errors and rectify wrongs. Self-judgment is generally a painful experience, for it necessitates the realization that we possess in our own personalities the negative traits that we condemn in others.

The Torah mandates, "You shall love your neighbor as yourself" (Leviticus 19:18). This means that self-respect is necessary in order to love another. Once a person esteems himself or herself as an object of love, then it is possible to express respect and love to another. Yet self-respect and self-love recognize internal deficiencies. A realistic self-appraisal delineates physical, moral, and social inadequacies. When we finally look inward into our own inner core, we locate patterns of error, self-righteous sins, and sometimes selfish acts which are morally reprehensible. Yet we find that we can live with ourselves. Despite our own failings, we still like ourselves. This then is what the Torah requires of all men—to treat others as we treat ourselves. Just as we love ourselves, even with our own problems and physical and moral blemishes, so too should we love and judge others. If we can disregard our own errors, so too should we disregard the failures of our friends.

Thus, the process of self-judgment has a practical moral component. It helps us to be more considerate and patient with others.

A whole year has fleetingly gone by, and numerous experiences are blurred by the passage of time. But one human characteristic is vibrant in our recollections. In the past year we were more concerned with our own interests than the needs of others. Our successes, our goals, our deals rather than the plight of our friends and neighbors. So on Rosh Hashanah, when we all stand in judgment before our Heavenly Father, we attempt to rectify this error. We Jews turn to our fellow Jew and wish them a *l'shanah tovah*. We pray that another person will be written and inscribed by God for a year of joy, happiness, health, and success. We know that by praying for our fellow man, not just mouthing rituals, we are manifesting repentance for past errors. We are showing our understanding of ourselves, our own failures, and our recognition that our neighbors are also worthy of value.

Tradition has it that "he who prays for his neighbor, and is in personal need of the same prayer, receives a favorable response from the Almighty prior to his neighbor."

L'shanah tovah. May all be written and inscribed for a year of love, joy, health, success, and continued commitment to Torah.

44. Yizkor: Jewish Destiny

The *Yizkor* service has a profound impact upon most people. It serves as a dynamic catalyst for the outpouring of a crescendo of emotions that dramatically mark our hearts and stir the memory chords of our souls.

It appears that nothing so saddens a man, so shakes a person's composure, as the fact of death. Perhaps it is because death pragmatically teaches us the futility of much of life itself.

A teacher of mine many years ago once shocked me by noting a bizarre revelation about his own personality. He said that upon returning from a funeral he had many times experienced the sensation of joy and personal pride. When questioned and probed as to how he could be so unfeeling, so ghastly, so inconsiderate of human emotions, he answered in the following fashion: "My pride, my joy, is that I'm alive and not dead. The same sickness, the same misfortune that befell my friend could have occurred to me. The same tragedy felt by his family could have been experienced by mine. But it didn't happen! The sickness and tragedy did not occur to me. I am alive. I am well. There must be a divine purpose in keeping me alive. God wants me to live. For this I'm happy. For this reason I have joy."

This anecdote has a pragmatic lesson to it. We chant *Yizkor* to memorialize the lives of beloved ones. We are saddened that they are no longer with us. No longer able to share our lives and enrich our experiences. But we must remember that there is a purpose to being alive. Everyone—all of us—are brought to this world to do something; to make some accomplishment. No one really knows the details of man's specific divine mission. Is it to be a great scholar and leader? Is it to develop a family of joy? To have a zest for living? Or to do just one simple good deed at the right time, to the right person?

The Talmud relates that a venerable sage had a dream that a lowly blacksmith was to be his partner in paradise. This bothered the rabbi. Here he was a man who studied Torah constantly, a person who tried to observe all that, indeed, should be observed, and who was to be his partner in paradise but a lowly, ignorant blacksmith, not known for his piety or leadership. The matter so disturbed the rabbi that he girded his courage to ask the blacksmith himself about his actions. He approached the man and mentioned that he had heard some wonderful things about him. But, the rabbi noted, he was interested in knowing what specific character trait he had that marked him as unique. The blacksmith answered that he had neither great education nor wonderful deeds. He was a simple person. But one thing he always did. Whenever he saw a person sad, he cheered him up. When he saw a disagreement amongst people, he created peace. The rabbi lifted his hands to God and prayed that he—the rabbi—should be worthy to sit in paradise next to such a holy man as the blacksmith.

We do not know the reward for specific good deeds and mitzvot. We do not know our mission in life. Our task is to do—to do good deeds and seek out our divine purpose in life.

A partial guide for the direction of our lives is to be noted in the story of Jonah, which is read on Yom Kippur in synagogues throughout the world. (Book of Jonah, Chap. 1.)

Jonah was a prophet commissioned by God to preach a prophecy of repentance to the people of Nineveh. God wanted Nineveh to serve as a model for the Jewish people: to demonstrate that just as the people of the sinful gentile city of Assyria could alter their ways and repent, so too could the Jews. But Jonah didn't like his task. He didn't want to go. He felt that it would be shameful for the Jews if gentiles were more religious and pious than they. So he ran away. He changed his name, changed his distinctive Jewish garb, altered his credentials, and booked a voyage to Tarshish. But can man run away from God? Can man run away from his own identity? Of course not. Jonah was identified, cast off the ship, swallowed by the proverbial whale, and directed to his destiny.

Today, many follow the path of Jonah. Many try to lose their Jewish identity. They refuse to accept the raison d'être of their own spiritual existence. Some years ago this was accomplished by the change of a name. Cohen became Conner or Collin, and Greenberg became Gray. Today it is no longer necessary to change a name in order to lose your religion. The modern mode is to merely make believe you're not a Jew. Just simply cast off all Jewish obligations. No one will bother you.

The only problem is that in times of social upheaval, pogroms, and war, it matters not whether your name is Cohen or Conner, Greenberg or Gray, whether you go to shul or not, whether religious or assimilated—the bell of destruction tolls for all of us. I have always felt that the completely assimilated Jew of Europe—the one who was ashamed to be called a Jew or to associate with Jews—his greatest shock was that no matter how he hid himself, no matter how he hated Jews and Judaism, the Nazis considered him a Jew—a peer of those East European Jews whom he himself hated. What an experience—what trauma!

Jews cannot always hide themselves. They are located. They are found. Sometimes our enemies find them. Sometimes we find ourselves.

Today, pogroms and overt anti-Semitism are not the major fear of American Jews. Today, the enemy is within us. "The fault, dear Brutus, is not in our stars, but in ourselves." We who fought for so many centuries to preserve our faith, our integrity, are voluntarily surrendering our religious values for the sake of convenience and luxury. It is too difficult to come regularly to shul. It is too costly to send children to yeshivot. It is not our problem that Jews are sick or in need. Charity begins at home. A new Cadillac is more important than a contribution to the Federation welfare fund. Shouldn't children be modern? What's wrong with a little interfaith dating? Why must we who believe ourselves to be good—why must we worry about the others? What's wrong? We are not walking but running away from our destiny. We are no longer the masters of our fate, but drifting without guidance.

A story is told of a king who was angry with his son. His son so incensed the king that he banished him from the palace and all royal possessions. The cast-off prince was forbidden to mention his royal pedigree and went about the countryside seeking sustenance. For years he vacillated from job to job, from occupation to occupation, to provide for his minimal basic needs. Finally, after much wandering, he made his home as a shepherd tending a flock of sheep. His master was kind to him, and he found happiness with the pastoral life. When the master died, he made the prince an equal partner with his son. The son, however, felt that the prince was an interloper and attempted to coerce the prince to leave his job and home. One day, by coincidence, the king happened to visit that small town. As custom had it, all were able to come before the king with petitions and pleas. The prince did not recognize his father, the king. He together with others came with a petition. He mournfully told his tale—that he had been promised land—and tearfully requested royal permission to remain in his home to continue to serve his sheep. Upon hearing the tale and the request, the king began to cry. How low has my son sunk that he forgets his own father? How low has he become that he forgets his royal pedigree? My son asks for sheep when he should ask for a kingdom.

This too is our problem today. We have forgotten our roots. We are divine messengers who have forgotten the message. We ask for health, for a roof over our family, for *parnassa*, when we should demand a kingdom. We come like beggars instead of like kings. We should request the return of the elevation of Israel and peace for the world.

But, as Jonah was found, so too are Jews found again. Jonah couldn't run away. Neither can Jews. We too have a destiny. We too find our ways back. An atheistic grandfather sires a *frum* grandson. A rebellious youth becomes a pillar of synagogue life. The *pintele yid*—the Jewish spark within us—sooner or later comes to the forefront. An Israel was created. Jewish education is on the upbeat. Synagogues now have young adults. Jewish life will never die. Everybody is found. Some sooner than others. Some in more intensive ways than others. Sometimes it takes a few generations. Some are found through death, some by tragedy, others through joy, and still others by accidents or coincidents of fate. Our royal pedigree will not be tarnished. Just as Jonah was found, so will we.

But how was Jonah found? Did he not hide his identity? Back to our tale.

The Almighty caused a storm to rock and shake the boat upon which Jonah was traveling. The seamen and passengers, quaking in fear over the safety of their lives, began to throw overboard all luggage and freight. It didn't help. The boat was floundering. It was about to capsize. Each man began to pray. Each in his own tongue and his own religion. As all were praying and crying, they noticed that one person was not there. One person was not praying. It was Jonah. Jonah was sleeping. He must be responsible! He must be the reason for the storm! If all try to achieve a goal, if all put all efforts into praying and requesting mercy, and nothing happens, it may mean that the man sleeping has the power to achieve the good needed. By his not praying he places all in jeopardy. Maybe it's Jonah's prayers that are needed. He's holding back divine help by sleeping. Yes, sometimes a man's destiny is faced by sleeping. Jonah was cast into the waters—and the boat was saved.

Today, we too pray. Our ships of fortune are also battling the storms of life. Sometimes we too feel that our ships are about to capsize. We need help. But who is holding up our prayers? Who is sleeping? Is it the little old woman, the dapper grandfather, the young businessman, the chic mother, the young adult sitting here in this synagogue sleeping, talking, not concerned with what is going on? From which person does God really demand prayer? Who is that person who has the power to save us all? Which one of us is Jonah? Jonah is here today. He may be Everyman.

45. Chanukah: A Modern Problem

In the popular mind, the tumultuous tale of Chanukah is a dynamic expression of the universal resistance to tyranny and the human quest for self-liberty. It is a document of war that begins with the vicious oppression by the Greek king Antiochus and concludes with the miraculous victory of the Maccabean freedom fighters. But Chanukah is certainly more than a heroic military tale. Indeed, such a description fails to accurately portray either the dire depths or the lofty aims of our rebellion. What then is the message of Chanukah?

Our talmudical sages refer to this historical epoch by calling it the age of the Greek Exile. Superficially, this classification appears to be inaccurate. The Jews were not in exile during the Greek oppression. They were living in their own homeland, in ancient Israel. They were not carted off to distant lands or dispersed throughout alien countries. Yet a more careful analysis shows that our sages are actually presenting the key toward a mature understanding of this entire era.

Historians record that after the initial painful pangs of a crushing military defeat, the full blessing of freedom and unlimited rights of citizenship were granted all who assimilated into the Greek culture and religion. Only those who were true to the laws of Judaism were persecuted and oppressed. As a result, great masses of Jews, rich and poor, educated and ignorant, publicly renounced their Jewish heritage in order to achieve political and economic favor. Renegade Jewish leaders preached pagan rites, and Jerusalem slowly became a bastion of Greek culture. Jews who practiced Judaism were strangers in their own homeland, foreigners in their own country.

This is what is meant by the term the "Greek Exile." Jews became aliens in their own land. Traditional laws, beliefs, and customs became downgraded and forgotten. The nation was estranged from its own heritage. In the schools, marketplaces, and seats of influence, it was Greek culture—not Jewish—that was studied, discussed, and enhanced. Judea became a Greek nation, not a Jewish one.

The Maccabees recognized that this cruel spiritual exile actually threatened the very core of our religious existence. The aim of the successful revolt was the recapture of the soul of the Jewish nation, to recrystallize the dignity of Jewish beliefs, and to once again make our beliefs and observances the pride and glory of Israel. The Maccabees won the war but failed to erase completely the corroding seeds of assimilation. This was a task left to each generation, to each community and home.

This is the message of Chanukah to Jews of our day. You were born a Jew, and a Jew you shall die. Will you live like one?

46. Al HaNisim

The *Al HaNisim* prayer chanted during Chanukah tersely delineates the essential historical aspects of the holiday. It states that subsequent to the Jewish military victory over the legions of Antiochus, the *Kohanim* cleansed and purified the *Bait HaMikdash*, kindled the lights, and established the eight days of Chanukah for purposes of thanksgiving and praise to the Almighty.

This suggests that the ancient Jews did not proclaim a religious celebration immediately after vanquishing their enemies; for the winning of a war is but an opportunity not an end in itself.

The Maccabean war was fought for religious freedom. The goal was an opportunity to observe Judaism without fear of bodily harm or social stigma. As a result, the primary concern was to cleanse and purify the Holy Temple. The cruse of oil that miraculously burned for eight days was a culmination of the dedication and purification of the *Bait HaMikdash*.

In other words, the focus of the Jewish people was the restoration of their Holy Temple and religious practises.

Today, this aspect of Chanukah is simply overlooked. Popular custom is to kindle the menorah and celebrate the Jewish freedom fighters of olden times.

Perhaps we should attempt to emulate the role of the Maccabees. Yes, there should be joy and celebration, but in addition, how meaningful it would be to utilize Chanukah as a vehicle to crystallize greater dedication to our synagogue, Torah institutions, and Israel.

Chanukah teaches us the message that freedom implies obligation. We are happy not just for the past, but because we have the opportunity to serve. Chanukah, therefore, is rooted in the present and the future. What a shame it is if the Jew sees joy only in his past.

47. Adar: The Increase of Joy

Purim is a holiday of joy. Its excitement so permeates our consciousness that the entire Hebrew month of Adar overlaps with happiness. Tradition has it that *Mishe'nichnas Adar marbin b'simcha*—"When the month of Adar arrives, one should increase happiness." (*Ta'anit* 29a). Of concern is that the Hebrew verb for "increase" (*marbin*) is written in the plural construct. Why should this be so? Why is the increase of happiness described solely as a plural entity?

Jews have a saying, "all beginnings are difficult." Again, the plural term is utilized. Is not the same meaning derived from the phrase "every beginning is difficult"? Why constantly the emphasis upon a multitude of events or emotions?

Most people believe that a new venture entails a unique start, a difficult process of development. What is at times not emphasized is that new concerns (business, religion, etc.) crystallize not one but many new vistas. There is no such thing as only one new event. The starting of something crystallizes a process of numerous new happenings. This is what the saying is imparting: when one embarks upon a new venture, realization should be directed to the fact that the obstacle to overcome is not one problem but numerous difficulties that emerge.

So too with joy. Happiness is not to be a fleeting sensation. A happy person is not one who has but one good happening. Happiness is the culminant positive sensation from numerous good experiences. This is the concern for the month of Adar.

Each Jew should endeavor to seek those activities that serve as a catalyst for a multitude of wonderful results. For that's real happiness. *L'chayyim* to life.

48. Purim: A Study of Anti-Semitism

Danger is not a unique experience to the Jew. Throughout our history numerous enemies have attempted to destroy our identity. We have been the victims of almost every conceivable physical torture and mental anguish known to man. Yet we have survived. We have survived, and our enemies have perished.

As a result, it is surprising that our victory in the time of Purim should receive so much prominence in Jewish lore. Why is it that Purim is singled out for festive celebrations and other Jewish victories are not? Was Haman of Persia the worst enemy of our people? Why does Halachah require that Purim must be celebrated by sending presents to friends, giving charity to the poor, and enjoying a festive meal? Should not this be required for every victory over our enemies?

The uniqueness of Purim lies not in the attempted annihilation of Jews, but, rather, in the motivation for such a brutal onslaught. Haman despised Mordecai. Everyone except Mordecai afforded Haman great honor and homage. It was Mordecai, the Jewish leader, who was the one thorn in Haman's egomaniacal thrust for power. This suggests a clue to the understanding of some anti-Jewish activities. The story of Purim articulates the principle that anti-Semitism may at times be a direct effect of personality problems. A personal clash of personalities may be the germ for subsequent ideological assaults upon our religion. A personal action perceived to be cruel may plant the seed for anti-Jewish pogroms.

138

The prominence of Purim is that the story sets the pattern for history by providing the classic charge levelled against our people. It instructs us to detect the repetitious nature of anti-Jewish activities throughout the ages of history and countries of our exile.

Haman was so disturbed over Mordecai's refusal to bow to him that Mordecai became symbolic of all that was hateful and threatening to his ambition.

To sustain his own image of grandeur, Haman connivingly devised a plan to destroy Mordecai. Mordecai, the person, was the true adversary of Haman. Yet Mordecai could not be directly attacked, nor his good name besmirched. Mordecai was popularly known as a loyalist of King Ahasuerus. Did not Mordecai inform the king of a plot to murder him? Was not Mordecai publicly honored for such information by the explicit directive of the king? No, Mordecai was too popular a person to be dealt with directly. The only way to destroy Mordecai was to include him within some general category of people manifesting antisocial behavior. If such antisocial behavior could be shown to threaten the stability of Persian social life, then revenge could be finally exacted upon Mordecai.

It does not pay to attack individual Jews. They are at times simply wonderful people. They are too well known as loyal, solid, reputable citizens to be valid targets of oppression. Better to discuss the group at large; better to find a social fault which may be falsely dramatized as a vile crime against society.

So Haman met with the king. He informed Ahasuerus of a major social problem disturbing the harmony of the king's reign.

"There is one nation, scattered and separated throughout the provinces of your kingdom; their customs are different from all others; they do not observe the decrees of the king; and there is no benefit for the king to sustain them" (free interpretation, Esther 3:8).

There is a nation that manifests peculiar social customs.

Instead of living together as a cohesive large unit and thus acquiring strength in their aggregate numbers, they are scattered throughout the provinces of the kingdom. Thus, no one area contains a sufficient quantity of Jews to be a military threat to the government. They are a minority wherever they reside. In addition, amongst themselves they are not organized under any structure or discipline. These people are "separated" from each other. For some reason they are not able to live together in harmony. This distinct separateness creates a band of antisocial individuals. Such a group can never be assimilated into the mainstream of Persian culture for two basic reasons. One, their culture is different from any other nation in the world. Two, they do not observe Persian cultural and political laws. What benefit is there to permit such an antisocial behavior to exist? If others were to follow such behavior, then Persian society would disintegrate. For which nation ruled by a king can stand idly by at the growth of anarchy? A people that is neither loyal to their government nor compatible with each other does not deserve compassion. Such a nation must be exterminated for the well-being of the general society at large.

At no time was the name of Mordecai ever mentioned by Haman. At no time was personal ambition ever discussed with the king. Haman, the crafty anti-Semite, simulated the role of the statesman seeking only the welfare of the king and the solidarity of the nation.

Thus, the story of Purim was not just a victory over enemies of the Jews. It was the forerunner of classic anti-Semitic principles. It was a dramatic guide to detect the evil guile inherent in so-called altruistic solutions to social problems.

Above all, it taught the Jew how Jewish self-hatred can be manipulated by our enemies to sustain Jewish annihilation. For this reason, it was decreed that Purim requires a distinct form of celebration. Jews cannot afford a life of separateness from each other. Jews were almost destroyed because of their inability to relate with harmony to each other. Jews must formally manifest patterns of love, friendship, and other intense inter-personal relationships. Therefore, on Purim, charity to the poor must be granted. *Shalach manot*—gifts to friends—must be sent. What better way is there to show appreciation to friends and compassion for the poor? Does this not interweave us all into the fine fabric of a cohesive community? Last but not least, a festive meal shared by family and friends is to be enjoyed. What finer way is there to show togetherness?

No generation is immune from anti-Semitism. Certainly not ours. Let us, on Purim at least, discard our petty differences, our ideological concerns for religious or Zionist purity, and our reasons for disagreeing with each other. Let us show the world that Jews are together. Let us demonstrate that we truly love our fellow Jew. Seek out the poor—seek out those we love; and those we don't. Let us give gifts to each other. Let us end our day in the company of friends at a festive religious feast.

Let us show the all-compassionate Father in Heaven that Jews are truly *am echad*, one nation: one people, one extended family.

49. The Relevance of Purim Gifts

A special feature of the Purim celebration is the mitzvah to send *shalach manot*—gifts to friends. Yet some rationale must be presented as to why this requirement is an integral aspect of only Purim and not other holidays. Should not this beautiful custom be associated with all religious commemorations of Jewish victory? To the extent that the mitzvah is exclusively limited to Purim, this suggests that the giving of gifts is a symbolic manifestation of the essential message of Purim itself.

In an attempt to persuade Ahasuerus of the necessity to destroy our people, Haman described Jews as being scattered throughout the 127 provinces with a religion distinct from all other nations (Esther 3:8). Yet it was only Mordecai, the religious Jew, who refused to bow to Haman. Why were all Jews to be grouped together for annihilation? Were all Jews religious in that era? Many of them were undoubtedly distinguished citizens of Persia, totally assimilated within the gentile culture. Great numbers attended the royal party in Shushan without an iota of concern as to whether or not it was kosher. It is most probable that Hebrew as a language was replaced by the Jews with local dialects or languages of each province.

This is the message of Purim. When an anti-Semitic Haman hates a Jew, all Jews are lumped together for destruction. The Haman binds all Jews by their religion. No one escapes. All are to be called Jews, whether they live by their religion or not. Hitler recreated this concept of genocide.

Purim is the story of Jewish vulnerability in the diaspora.

142

When a pogrom crystallizes, no Jew is safe. Even those who voluntarily surrender their Judaism are marked as objects for tyranny. The hatred of an anti-Semite is all-embracing and nonselective in nature. When one Jew is attacked (religious or nonreligious) all Jews may be in jeopardy.

It is for this reason that *shalach manot* gifts were instituted as a means of celebrating the victory over only Haman and his evil decrees. The sages wished to emphasize that Jewish unity should not only be a phase of danger but also of peace. Each Jew should be aware of his bond with his correligionists, not just to fight a common enemy or experience persecution, but to share in prosperity and joy. The fate of a Jew in diaspora is inextricably bound together with his nation. We are all vulnerable, and therefore we must all appreciate the necessity of friendship and bonds of Jewish brotherhood. The giving of gifts is a token expression of love and togetherness. Each Jew shares something with his friend. We dramatically demonstrate to all that Jewish survival depends on Jewish unity; and that Jewish unity has a positive value in times of peace.

That is what Purim is all about. The Jewish existence depends upon all of us. Let us start loving Jews. *L'chayyim*—to life. It is our life that needs unity.

50. The Purim Seudah

In ancient Shushan, Haman planned a brutal genocide of the Jewish people. Men, women, and children were to be destroyed. Jews were not granted an opportunity to escape by assimilating or converting to a pagan lifestyle. The objective was comparable to the aims of the Third Reich. The land was to be freed from Jews. Thus, the story of Purim did not entail a *kulturkampf* of ideological or spiritual values.

The sages, therefore, made it a mitzvah to have a *seudah* (festival meal) on Purim to manifest the deliverance from physical harm by a requirement to celebrate the enjoyment of physical pleasure.

What is of special interest is the halachic requirement for the mitzvah of the Purim *seudah* to be observed only by day and not by night. Why? Do not Jews calculate a calendar date change by the night prior to the day? Does not Shabbat commence on Friday evening and not on Saturday morning? If so, then why should not Jews be able to observe the mitzvah of the *seudah* on the night of Purim?

The Talmud relates that it is prohibited to eat a meal prior to the feeding of one's animals (*Berachot* 40a). The implication of this humane ruling is that such animals are dependent upon their owner for sustenance. As a result, it is immoral to make them wait helplessly for food while their owner sustains his personal needs. In such a case, the personal desires of the owner take second place to the needs of such animals who are his responsibility to feed.

144

A general moral rule may be gleaned from this particular law. If such care is to be extended to animals, how much more so should it apply to people. This suggests that if a person is responsible for the survival of another, perhaps it also would be prohibited to eat prior to making certain that such person is sustained properly. In other words, personal gratification is only permitted after one has met his obligation to care for those who await his help.

On Purim each Jew is required to give charity to two poor individuals. Such people, because of their poverty, cannot enjoy the festivity of the holiday unless someone extends to them a donation. They are aware that on Purim charity will be granted. As a result they await with anticipation for some kind donor to sustain their needs.

For this reason, perhaps, the Purim *seudah* is not celebrated on the night of Purim. The sages felt that it would be sacrilegious to permit festive meals while the poor are yet hungry. Only by day may it be observed. This way there is enough time to enable all to care for the poor and the needy, so that when the Jew finally partakes of his meal to celebrate his physical survival, he knows that those who look to him for support— they too are cared for. Only then may the Jew enjoy his meal. *L'chayyim.*

51. Redemption

Jews celebrate freedom from Egyptian bondage on Passover. At the Seder, which is on the first night of the holiday, we laud our deliverance, and numerous rituals dramatically and symbolically transport us thousands of years to the lifestyle of an ancient past. We act as if we ourselves were freed from slavery.

But were we actually free at that period of time? The Talmud (*Megillah* 14a) notes that the Jews chanted *Hallel* (Praise to the Lord) at their status transformation from slavery to freedom. Rashi contends that this occurred by the miracle of the Red Sea. Accordingly, when the enemies were destroyed, the Jews were so elated that they spontaneously sang a song of praise to God. This suggests that the true sense of freedom occurred on the seventh day of Passover. Only when the Egyptian soldiers were destroyed did the Jewish people really feel free enough to express their joy of thanksgiving. If so, then the major ritual celebration of Jewish freedom should take place on the seventh day of Passover and not on the eve of the first day. It is difficult to consider the ancient Jews free prior to the crossing of the Red Sea. They departed from Egypt. But shortly they were besieged by the Egyptian army. They were confused, bewildered, and frightened. Is this the freedom we celebrate? A one-night elation to be subsequently transformed into a potential national calamity? Should not the Seder, therefore, take place on the seventh day of Passover? A time of communal bliss; an era of future-directed action; a period wherein all enemies are destroyed and fear dissipated.

This suggests that the Seder night does not necessarily commemorate freedom per se but, rather, something else.

The Talmud (*Berachot* 9a) contends that redemption (*g'oola*) occurred the (first) *night* of Passover, and the (actual) exodus took place by *day*. Rashi defines redemption as "permission to depart."

Thus, three major events took place. (1) Redemption (at night), (2) exodus (by day), and (3) freedom (on the seventh day).

The Seder does not celebrate freedom but, rather, redemption. Freedom from enemies is not a realistic status. It is messianic in nature. Every generation has its share of anti-Semites. Every era in history has its Jewish pogroms. The Jew is to be rooted in reality. Our people revere miracles but do not rely upon them to guide our lives.

We celebrate, rather, redemption. The Jew has permission (authority) to depart from his bondage. We may be surrounded by enemies—but we can leave them and "do our own thing." In Egypt, it was a courageous act of faith to depart from the land. The proclamation that we have "permission to leave" was a psychological force of strength. No one can enslave us. We can leave Egypt. Only God is our Lord. Whether we actually do depart—that is a matter of faith in our future.

For this reason, the Haggadah states that the *rasha* (the nonbelieving son) is told that had he been in Egypt, "he would not have been redeemed." Why? Because he would not have acted upon a mere "permission to leave." He would have viewed the might of Egypt, realized his potential danger, and then have been paralyzed with fear.

The Jew celebrates redemption each year. He recalls that he possesses the inner ability to seek freedom. It is within him. No man can give him that right. It is his birthright. He can live or depart from any nation. He can leave any situation. Any bondage is transitory. He has permission from God, not from man. He celebrates not the annihilation of enemies but the unshackling of bonds. The spirit of tomorrow permeates his presence. He and his people need not fear existing enemies. He is redeemed.

52. Talking About Freedom

The Haggadah states that "whoever endeavors to recite at length the story of the Exodus from Egypt is deemed praiseworthy." Thus it is meritorious to expand the quantitative recital of the Exodus during the celebration of the Pesach Sedarim. Yet why should this be so? There are other mitzvot in the Torah that are mandated to be remembered yet have no rule appended to them encouraging quantitative discussion.

For example, Jews are required by biblical statute to remember the Shabbat and the war initiated by Amalek. Yet by these mitzvot there is no suggestion that an increased recitation generates a unique status of praise.

Indeed, the very fact that the classification of being praiseworthy is granted to those who continue to dwell at length on the story of the Exodus suggests that the ultimate realization of this concept would be the total utilization of the entire night devoted to Pesach. For any moment or hour used for sleep or for non-Passover matters detracts from the amount of time available for yet further expansion on the tale of the Exodus. For this reason, the Haggadah relates the incident of the great sages who became so involved with this aspect of the mitzvah that they lost track of time and halted their discussion only when their students informed them that it was morning and the time for prayers. In other words, the rabbis observed the maximum quantitative dimensions of the mitzvah.

Yet it is necessary to seek the motivation for this unique religious rule. The Talmud (*Berachot* 13a) notes the following psychological maxim:

148

"A man was traveling on the road when he encountered a wolf and escaped from it, and he went along relating the story of the wolf. He then encountered a lion and escaped from it, and went along relating the affair of the lion. He then encountered a snake and escaped from it, whereupon he forgot the two previous incidents and went along relating the affair of the snake. So with Israel; *the later troubles make them forget the earlier ones.*"

This concept is so true. People tend to dwell on recent troubles and to forget the problems of the past. They talk about that which is most current and relevant. It is the contemporary issue that bothers people, not ancient history. In fact, when Jews talk about national calamities, the major concern is, of course, the tragedy of the Holocaust or more recently the enmity of the Arabs and the wars against Israel. Who worries about the Egyptian bondage? Who really cares about the Egyptian attempts at Jewish genocide when relatives and friends were brutally murdered by the Germans or the PLO? Do not people discuss that which is important to them and neglect that which is of no meaningful relevance?

For this reason the Haggadah tells us that it is praiseworthy to expand on the tale of the Egyptian bondage. Anyone who can shelve the memories of the atrocities of the present and concentrate solely upon the story of Egyptian bondage is truly praiseworthy. It is the story of the birth of our people. Our true independence. Anyone who can spend time forgetting the brutality of the Holocaust and transcends all present problems to relive our freedom tale—that person is meritorious; that person is worthy of praise. The more time one can devote to our season of freedom, the more merit one has. It is a dramatic reminder that present tragedies do not depress our soul. We can overcome all. It can be done. The rabbis of the Haggadah witnessed the terrible destruction of our land and yet were able to forget for a night the present to devote discussion to our past. So too with us.

This is the message of Pesach. Whoever can transcend present *tzores* to dwell upon our religious past will be blessed in the future. *L'shana haba'ah*—next year we will be free. The Jew is never immobilized because of his present. *L'shana haba'ah*—next year—Jerusalem.

53. Passover Seminar

We Jews do not live in a vacuum of values. We have roots. Roots that bind us to the past. Roots that give meaning to the present and hope for the future. Our religion serves as a potent reminder to reflect upon the direction of our daily, busy, patterns of life activity. Most people become so preoccupied with habit that the true meaning of our life becomes neglected. We become so obsessed with details that we lack the time to review the status of essential human values.

It is for this reason that Jewish law does not leave introspection and reflection to the whim of man. The Jew is busy. There are too many business obligations, social functions, and family problems to permit the leisure of self-evaluation. There always appears time to judge others, but never time to judge ourselves.

The Torah, therefore, mandates that once a year, eight days must be set apart as a seminar for freedom. The Jew is not requested to rethink the values of freedom, but, rather, to relive our past. Judaism is a religion of experience. Passover is a total immersion into the historicity of the Jew. For eight days we simulate the trauma of slavery and the bliss of redemption. We become slaves in Egypt. We personally eat their meals. We relive the horror. We, not just our ancestors, are personally freed from bondage.

Freedom and national goals now take on a new meaning. We have a frame of reference to view our present. We have been at the depths of human deprivation. Now we can better assess the value of human, religious, and personal freedom.

This is what Passover is all about. This is its inner meaning. This is the reason for the numerous mitzvot.

151

54. Passover: A Source of Beauty

The slavery was over. Pharaoh and his army were destroyed in the Red Sea. The humiliating, backbreaking subjugation to Egyptian taskmasters was but a memory of the past. Jews now had freedom. To express their joy in independence and devotion to the Lord, they immediately sung a song to the Almighty.

In that song they said, "This is my God and I will adorn Him." (Exodus 15:2). Commenting upon this biblical verse, our sages maintain that the means of adorning our Lord is by beautifying, enhancing, and embellishing all rituals and commandments. Thus it appears that the whole concept of religious service through beauty is derived from an occurrence related to the exodus from Egyptian bondage. This relationship implies that an analysis of the Jewish attitude toward Passover will shed light on the traditional meaning of beauty itself.

On Passover there is a specific commandment to relate all the wondrous events that led to our deliverance. The purpose is not to show the power of the Almighty by a detailed account of miraculous events. Indeed, such an attempt would even border upon the sacrilegious, for any list of man would by nature be limited. It is rather a means of recognizing the good, redeeming acts of grace which our Lord performed in our behalf. It is a process of showing our appreciation for the acts of deliverance. A means of saying "thank you" for being free. By reliving the pangs of our servile past, we are better able to dramatically feel the real joys of our present freedom.

Just as the concept of appreciation is the key to Passover observance, so too is it the underlying quality of beauty itself. If one is concerned with an item and considers it to be valuable, one will strive to beautify and enhance it. A beautiful object, in the traditional Jewish sense, is an object that possesses qualities of attraction that are appreciated by man. To beautify an item means to construct or clothe it so that favorable responses will be elicited.

Thus, the process of adorning ritual commandments with items of beauty is but an overt, active way of displaying our inner concern and appreciation for divine law.

On Passover, we Jews must intertwine into the fine fabric of our ritual observances the dual concepts of appreciation and beauty. Just as our ancestors thanked God for the miracle of the Red Sea, so too must we manifest our emotional concern by words of praise, songs of cheer, and items of value. By beautifying our Seder, by endowing the ritual with the best within us, we actively show how deeply we value our religious heritage.

It is hoped that on the Seder nights we Jews will feel the need to discuss the personal aspects of life that are usually taken for granted. I pray that all will firmly recognize the wonderful divine gift of life itself, and will find ways of both appreciating and beautifying it.

55. The Debt of Passover

The Haggadah informs us that had the Almighty not miraculously delivered our forefathers from Egypt, then even "we, our children, and our grandchildren would still be subjugated to Pharaoh." This statement is incredible to the modern mind, for such continual servitude is contrary to historical facts. Have not other nations been released from bondage? Does not the history of the world in the past twenty years demonstrate the potency of national freedom movements? If the Third World nations have achieved their liberty, could not the Jews also have acquired freedom?

The answer is that in time Jews also would have been freed from servitude. In fact, Pharaoh would have set them free. Jews would have been so overwhelmed with appreciation that each year a holiday would have been set aside to thank Pharaoh for his gracious liberalism. Pharaoh's Day would be celebrated like Lincoln's birthday. Imagine the pomp, ritual, and festivities that would be developed to enhance the image of Pharaoh and Egypt.

This is what the Haggadah is forewarning. Pesach is a time to thank God, not man. For if the Almighty had not saved our people, an Egyptian would have. Then, who knows how many generations of Jews would have been subjugated and beholden to Egyptian culture?

This is what Jewish freedom is all about. Our debt is to God, not man, and Pesach is a holiday to express this appreciation.

56. Emulating the Process of Sinai: A Torah Analysis

Jews are keenly aware that *Berachot* (blessings) are chanted prior to the performance of mitzvot. Just as a *berachah* is required before the sounding of the shofar or the wearing of tefillin, so too is a *berachah* mandated before the learning of Torah.

Yet not all forms of learning Torah require a *berachah*. The *Shulchan Aruch* specifically rules that should a person just think about Torah—without any oral vocalization—such a process does not need a *berachah* (*Orach Chayyim* 47:4). This law is challenged by the Vilna Gaon, who notes that Torah learning is not restricted to an oral, vocal process. Indeed, the rationale for such a ruling requires analysis. Is not intense thought a key ingredient necessary for the acquisition of knowledge? Torah learning is not an empty ritual to be studied by rote devoid of comprehension. As one attains a high degree of scholarship, it is vital to logically and coherently think through issues.

Indeed, according to the ruling of the codes the following bizarre case may develop. A young child may repeat but one verse of Scripture and be required to chant a *berachah*. A venerable sage may ponder a Torah problem affecting the lives of an entire community and not be charged with a *berachah* for such efforts. Whose Torah is greater? Also, the codes specifically note that the vehicle of writing Torah does require a *berachah* (ibid.). Why? Why is writing Torah more important than thinking Torah thoughts?

155

A basic response is that traditionally a *berachah* precedes an action. Since the process of contemplation is not an action, therefore no *berachah* was mandated. Thus the lack of a *berachah* is not a statement regarding the value of the thought process to Torah.

An alternate response is that the ruling of the codes alludes to an essential concept that permeates the purpose of Torah education.

Torah is not just a form of knowledge. It is a religious interlocking bridge paved to the past, lived in the present, and directed to the future. It is *mesorah*—a way of life transmitted in the past from generation to generation with the understanding that it will be given to our children to recreate further links to the future.

Perhaps, this is the true meaning of the Halachah that requires a *berachah* only for oral or written Torah; for only through such a process may Torah be transmitted to another generation. Torah solely within one's mind may be vastly creative, analytic, and brilliant—but it remains within the individual. No one can hear such thoughts. Torah learning should emulate the tradition of Sinai. In *Pirke Avot* it reads, "Moshe accepted the Torah from Sinai and transmitted it to Joshua, and Joshua to the elders—and they [gave it] to the prophets, who transmitted it to the men of the Great Assembly" (1:1). In other words, Torah is a gift that must be granted to others. It is not proper to obtain personal knowledge and to subsequently jealously guard such information solely for one's personal gratification. Torah has a dual responsibility. It must be learned and it must be taught. Oral or written Torah may be overheard or studied by another.

A *berachah* for Torah learning is required only when the process emulates the tradition of Sinai. Only such Torah which intertwines *mesorah* into its core is the type of Torah that merits a *berachah*.

This is what Shavuot is all about. It is not just a holiday to commemorate that Torah was given on Sinai, but also to recall that it was received by *K'lal Yisrael*.

The duality of Torah must be reenacted in each age. Each Jew must receive the benefits of Torah and strive to share with another.

57. Mount Sinai Today

Shavuot commemorates the Divine Revelation of the Torah on Mount Sinai. Rav Yehuda Halevi, the noted medieval poet and philosopher, suggests in the *Kuzari* that this awe-inspiring event distinguishes the Jewish people from all other religions.

A review of the origin of popular modern-day religion manifests that its source is shrouded in secrecy and garbed in a private, personal relationship. A man is said to have alone witnessed a spiritual experience which crystallizes into a "calling" to teach certain values to others. Not so the Jewish people. Our Torah was not given to one person, nor was it revealed in secrecy. Over 600,000 men, women, and children spiritually served as witnesses to this divine event. Torah was a national, social, historical experience. Every Jew had the role of a prophet.

This is the message of Shavuot to Jews of our age. Torah is not the exclusive domain of the rabbi or the teacher. Religious values are not limited to the spiritually pure and the pious amongst us. Torah and Judaism are the heirlooms of our national character. Every Jew is a potential Moshe Rabbenu, every child, a future Hillel.

We became a nation through Torah. It is, therefore, through the study of Torah that we reaffirm our national pride.

III. Torah and General Studies

58. The Loss of a Torah Sage
A Tribute to HaGaon Rav Yitzchok Hutner

Los Angeles is over 3,000 miles away from the major bastions of Torah leadership in New York City; Israel, an additional 7,000 miles distance. Yet, when the tragic news reached Los Angeles that Moreinu v'Rabeinu HaGaon HaRav R. Yitzchok Hutner (z.l.) had passed away in Jerusalem, thousands of miles of physical space and over twenty years of lapsed time all dissolved. Within my mind were images which transcended both space and time. I found myself reliving the past as vivid memories transplanted me as a yeshiva student in the actual presence of the Rosh HaYeshivah (rabbinical dean) once again.

The years were the late 1950s and early 1960s. The place— 350 Stone Avenue, the imposing seven-story former bank in the Brownsville section of Brooklyn, New York, which housed the Mesivta Rabbi Chaim Berlin Rabbinical Academy.

The era when, I feel, Chaim Berlin was at its apex as the most exciting yeshivah in America. Many institutions studied Torah. But none had such a dynamic, magnetic, controversial Rosh HaYeshivah as the Rosh HaYeshivah of Chaim Berlin. Other rabbis taught Torah. Rav Hutner (z.l.) created disciples. He was not just a leading member of the professional staff of the institution. He was the yeshivah. It was his creative imprimatur which uniquely molded the posture of the student body and through them the stature of American Torah scholarship.

Who was this rabbi? Why is his death any more tragic than

161

the loss of any Jewish leader? Why is it necessary to delineate the dimensions of his lifestyle, and the patterns of his leadership.

Rav Hutner was not just a great leader or scholar. He was a Torah giant. A Torah titan acclaimed as one of the true great men of our age.

Torah is not just an intellectual discipline or an emotional behavior. It is a "way of life" that cannot be acquired without a teacher. The basis of Torah is not knowledge but *mesorah* (tradition)—the transmission of sacred values from one era to another, from one person to another. This process requires not only the desire to learn but also the ability coupled with the will to transmit. A Torah personality can only be evolved through the dynamics of a *rebbe–talmid*, master-disciple relationship. This concept is the core of Rashi's first commentary in Genesis. Why, Rashi probes, did the Bible start with the story of creation? Why not with the first commandment that Jews were mandated to observe? Essentially, the question is a request for a basic definition of Judaism, namely, what is the nature of Torah? If it is but a compilation of divine commandments, then stories of the creation and heroes are extraneous. The true response is that Torah, being a way of life, cannot be taught in a vacuum of life conditions. It requires the history of heroes who serve as models for emulation. We do not learn Torah, but *Torat Moshe*. We study a discipline that men lived and personally transplanted to others. We have spiritual fathers. Without the process of a *rebbe–talmid* relationship, Torah would not differ from other religious experiences or intellectual disciplines. The positive on-going tension of the master–student relationship recreates the aura of *mesora*—the transmission of Torah in its pristine form. Was not Abraham beloved by the Almighty because he transplanted the seeds of justice and righteousness in his children, and through them, all future generations (see Genesis 18:19)? This is what Torah is all about. Knowledge can be learned, *Mesorah* must be taught. *Mesorah* requires a *rebbe*.

The genious of the Rosh HaYeshiva (z.l.) was in the uniqueness of the *mesorah* he promulgated. A *mesorah* that crystallized the primacy of Torah; the establishment of Torah personalities; and the mechanics for ensuring a new generation of Torah transmitters. Over 20,000 mourners attended his funeral in Jerusalem with less than several hours notice; rabbinical leaders mourned throughout the world—for his death marked the end of an era: the passing of a true transmitter of Torah—*mesorah*. His lifestyle as a teacher is truly a seminar in the developmental techniques for recreating Torah in our age.

I view the Rosh HaYeshivah in my mind's picture not at a public gathering but rather in the role of a personal guide to his students seated in his office engaged in a dialogue with a disciple. In fact, one hardly ever noted the Rosh HaYeshivah standing. He sat when he gave a *sheur* (class), he sat when he presented a public lecture. He commented upon this once by noting that there is a popular adage that "one stands and talks but sits and learns." Since all his discourses were in the realm of Torah education, he preferred to sit and thus emphasize the Torah framework of his address.

I do not recall him as an old man nor as he looked quite recently. I see him now as he appeared in his prime. He had jet black hair, a long gray beard, and eyes that simultaneously pierced and sparkled with intensity. His eyes gave the impression that he was not only observing you but gazing at the innards of one's soul. He was of medium height, stout, and wore a long black rabbinical frock with a massive black hat. He typified the image of a European rabbinic scholar. Yet, as a young student, he dressed in modern garb. As a yeshivah student in the famed European Slabodka Yeshivah his brilliant, incisive mind earned him the sobriquet of the *elliui* (prodigy) from Warsaw. He further received, at quite a young age, acclaim from the great Torah scholars of his era by the publication of his talmudic commentaries entitled *Torat HaNazir*. Yet he also attended the University of Berlin. He was well versed in psychology, philosophy, history, and poetry, especially the works of Byron. He was a synthesis of both Torah and secular wisdom. Yet, as Rosh HaYeshivah he gave the appearance of a Torah sage who outwardly seemed alien to all forms of modernity and secularism. In Slabodka he looked like a man of the world—in New York City he exuded the image of a *tzadik*. Something traumatic happened to him that affected his lifestyle; that trauma was *Eretz Yisrael*. Therein he became a devotee of Rav Kook, the Chief Rabbi, and an ardent student of the esoteric mystics of the Holy Land.

In a spirit of candor, he once informed me of the following incident. During his stay in *Eretz Yisrael* (he never referred to the Holy Land as Israel but always as *Eretz Yisrael)* he visited a kibbutz. Several young children alarmed the entire community by screeching, "Arabs are coming." It subsequently was noted that instead of Arabs, two Chassiddic Jews had entered the kibbutz. The Rosh HaYeshivah was perplexed and questioned the children as to the motivation for their assumption that these Chassidic Jews were Arabs. The children responded by saying, "They looked so different. They had long scraggly beards, strange coats, and peculiar-looking earlocks *(pe'ot)*." The Rosh HaYeshivah then told me that he realized that our children were tragically forgetting the traditional garb of the pious Jews, Rabbonim, and Chassidim. Just as we are proud of our culture, so too should we be proud of our distinctive garb. He pulled out his earlocks *(pe'ot)* from behind his ears and held them out to me. "All people have hair. But only Jews wear *pe'ot*." He stretched out his hand and gathered the bottom corner of his frock, "All men wear jackets," he said, "but only Jews wear such long coats. The *pe'ot* and the long frock are especially dear to me, for they distinctively show my Jewishness. I am proud to look like a Jew."

This anecdote typifies the Rosh HaYeshivah: dramatic, stark, incisive, yet original.

It was said in the late 1950s that there were three major

distinctive Chassidic yeshivot in New York. Chabad-Lubavitch was a Chassidic yeshivah, for both the rebbe and the students were Chassidim. Torah Vadaat was a Chassidic yeshivah, for a majority of the student body came from Chassidic homes. Chaim Berlin was a Chassidic yeshivah, even though the student body was primarily from American homes, for the Rosh HaYeshivah simulated the role of a Chassidic rebbe. How true.

Rav Hutner (z.l.) gathered around him a coterie of dedicated disciples who manifested the same ardor, devotion, submission, and militancy that any Chassid manifested in behalf of his Rebbe. This cadre of disciples was a heterogeneous combination of dissimilar types who shared two essential qualities. One, they were devoted to the Rosh HaYeshivh. Two, each displayed some mark of excellence; some unique characteristic that the Rosh HaYeshivah treasured. The brilliant Torah students gained entree to this select group by the sheer power of their Torah knowledge. Those who were not great student scholars but exemplified unusually pious behavior could utilize piety as their entree. Others, who lacked the above qualities yet excelled in specific secular disciplines of wisdom as well as music, were also granted an opportunity to serve as peers of this unit.

In effect, the Rosh HaYeshivah created a feudal court of unusually brilliant students who were masters of diversified fields of endeavor.

The yeshiva had over 300 full-time Bait HaMedresh students from post–high school age to married men in their thirties. Not all ever developed a personal, intimate relationship with the Rosh HaYeshivah. Many simply learned Torah, attended classes, seminars, lectures comparable to other rabbinical academies. They were simply yeshivah students. Those, however, privileged to join the Rosh HaYeshivah's inner circle—they were potential disciples. They had the benefit of being involved in the dynamics of a *rebbe–talmid* relationship that would mark their attitudinal and behavioral patterns for life. This fact served as a magnet to attract gifted students to Chaim Berlin. Though Rav Hutner cared for all his students, he had a genius for discerning potential and for molding good raw student material to heights of stature. To Rav Hutner (z.l.) the adage that "whosoever teaches Torah to the child of his friend is comparable to having given birth to him" was more than a talmudic citation, it was the essence of his Torah personality. He was not a teacher of students. He was their father. Torah, he noted, was uniquely different from other attainments. Technical knowledge can be acquired from numerous sources. Torah was equated to life, and just as life can only be derived from parents, so too must Torah be created from a process that simulates parenthood. The Torah teacher, therefore, is in fact the spiritual father of the child.

The first portion of the *Shema* states, *V'sheenantam l'vanecha*— "and you shall teach them [Torah] to your children" (Deut. 6:7). The Rambam defines this scriptural verse to be an obligation to teach Torah to students, for students are considered children (see Rambam, *Laws of Talmud Torah*, chap. 1). The Rosh Ha-Yeshivah defined this concept as follows: The verse is not suggesting that Torah must be taught to students who incidentally are also called children. The Rambam is, rather, articulating the principle that the process of teaching Torah creates the status of children. Parenthood is necessary for the creation of life. The Torah parent, the teacher, fuses students with the potency of Torah and thus creates children. Anyone who does not so create children of Torah fails in his role as a teacher.

Teaching Torah had an additional dimension of value to the Rosh HaYeshivah which was articulated by a distinction made between an inheritance and a sale. A sale represents a transfer of possession and ownership between two entities. Once a sale is legally transacted, no relationship exists between the present owner and the former owner. An inheritance, however, represents more than just a transfer of ownership. The person who inherits, for example, property from his father, perpetuates the original identity of his father. The son symbolically serves as a replacement for his father. The father lives through the service of the child. "The Torah that Moses commanded us is an inheritance to the congregation of Jacob" (Deut. 33:4). Torah is an act of inheritance. The *rebbe* lives through the inheritance of his student. Torah creates children and in the process is a vehicle for the renewal of the *rebbe's* values. In effect, the master recreates his own life through the creation of disciples.

Rav Hutner (z.l.) served as the father of his disciples. Apart from his preholiday lectures, he hardly ever spent time in the Beth HaMedresh. Almost always was he in his office meeting privately with students. Each person developed according to his unique talents and potentiality. The scope of the dialogues was indeed broad. To some it was pure Torah; brilliant discourses in Talmud, Halacha, ethics, or ideology. To others—an anaylsis of a philosophical concept or a psychological problem. To still others—the development of attitudes and conceptions of life. Each student was treated as if he were the personal "apple of the eye" of the Rosh HaYeshivah. Each person's problems were considered the most important concerns in the world. All discussions were based on the Slabodka theory that each person is the master of his universe. Each student was a potential leader. Each was imbued with the seed of greatness that must flower to fruition.

To the extent that the Rosh HaYeshivah actually believed that he was the father of his students, he felt it was his obligation to know their total personality. No subject matter was extraneous to his purview. What a student did in life, whom he married or intended to marry, and where he lived—all were proper matters of intense concern to the Rosh HaYeshivah. No student, however, was permitted while still in the yeshivah to diminish this special relationship. I recall vividly an incident wherein a favored student had sent an invitation to his wedding to the Rosh HaYeshivah. The student was summoned to a personal interview and asked whether he had sent an invitation to his father. "Of course not," said the student, "he's my father. He's part of the wedding. I didn't send him an invitation." "So," said the Rosh HaYeshivah, "why do you humiliate me by treating me in a lesser fashion than your father?"

The Rosh HaYeshivah believed that *kavod haTorah*—the honor due Torah—was essential for learning Torah properly. Just as tradition has it that true *kavod* (honor) is found in Torah, so too must it be in reverse, that lack of dignity or disrespect negates the efficacy of Torah. Rav Hutner (z.l.) was a stickler for proper modes of respect. No one ever addressed him directly by name or by a pronoun. He was always referred to in the third person, as the "Rosh HaYeshivah." No student ever left his presence by turning his back to the Rosh HaYeshivah and walking frontwards toward the door. The student would, rather, face the Rosh HaYeshivah and walk humbly backwards till his exit. When the Rosh HaYeshivah was invited to a festive occasion, such as the wedding of a student, it was necessary to provide personal transportation. No student would ever meet the Rosh HaYeshivah unless he was properly dressed. This, of course, mandated the wearing of a jacket.

In terms of directives, no student ever openly disputed his decisions. Yet the Rosh HaYeshivah did not inform a student directly what actions should be taken. He discussed options. His directives were presented only in instances when he knew they would be obeyed. It is related that a student once informed the Rosh HaYeshivah of his intention to visit *Eretz Yisrael*. The Rosh HaYeshivah responded to him as follows: "If your decision is to leave, then I extend a blessing that all should be well. If, however, your desire is to request my thoughts on the matter, then please be aware that I will not inform you of them, unless you grant me your word that you will follow my directive."

Rav Hutner (z.l.) had a special fondness for music. He even composed numerous melodies that he sang with verve on holidays or festive occasions. His robust, booming, yet melodious voice would infuse the entire yeshivah with an inspiration to join together and lose themselves in the ecstasy of song (n'gina). He also utilized music as a vehicle to crystallize a special attitudinal and emotional aura for his ethical discourses. Once we gathered in a lecture hall for a private seminar. The room had no lights and the sun was about to set. As twilight slowly evolved into the darkness of night, from a corridor could be heard the soft sad sounds of a violin playing the contemplative strains of the "Rav's Niggun," that intricately beautiful melody composed by Rav Shneur of Lyadi, the outstanding founder of the Chassidic Chabad movement. (The violinist was a yeshivah student who was also an outstanding student at the famed Juilliard School of Music.) As pitch-black darkness set upon us, the music stopped. At that moment, the Rosh HaYeshivah began his ethical discourse. Every student present, I am positive, experienced heights of religious contemplation. All were extremely receptive to the Torah lecture.

The major role of the Rosh HaYeshivah was not just to teach Torah (that others could do) but to crystallize the formation of a Torah personality. A person whose perspective is imbued with Torah regardless of profession or endeavor.

He once presented the following dilemma. Two students are learning in a yeshivah. One student learns extremely well by day and by night attends a secular college. The other is a poor student, not diligent in his studies, yet devotes his full time to the yeshivah. Which student is closer to the ideals of Torah? An initial reaction would be that the diligent student is, of course, better than the nondiligent one. That, suggested the Rosh Ha-Yeshivah, is not necessarily a keen perception of the attitudes of both students. In terms of knowledge, the diligent student is on a higher level than his friend. He simply knows more than the other. But in terms of a Torah personality, the weaker student surpasses the other. The college student has a dichotomy of values. Torah is important and must be studied. But so too are secular studies. In terms of values both disciplines appear on an equal plane. The *batlan,* the weaker student, has only one value, Torah. Ask him what is important in life and his response will be only Torah. The fact that he personally does not discipline himself to better utilize his time is a personal inadequacy but not a value judgment on the lack of the importance of Torah.

Secular studies were never denigrated by the Rosh Ha-Yeshivah. They were not considered in the realm of prohibited information. He recognized full well the need for students to make a living in the world at large. He knew full well that not all could succeed solely as devotees of Torah. But he insisted on delineating the proper perspective of Torah to all other disciplines. All secular knowledge, he felt, was a mass of zeroes. By themselves, not worth anything. Torah is the numeral one. When it is placed before all the zeroes, then—and only then—do they amount to a substance of value.

Torah knowledge is not an attainment but, rather, an essential ingredient of the character of the Jews. The Rosh Ha-Yeshivah noted that both Torah and secular wisdom are extolled by Halachah (Jewish law). The codes mandate a special blessing to be chanted upon observing a great Jewish scholar renowned for Torah. The codes, moreover, also require a unique blessing to be chanted upon meeting a great gentile scholar noted for his wisdom (*Orech Chayyim* 224:6, 7). The implication is that a Jew known for his secular wisdom (not Torah) does not mandate a blessing. Why? In the laws of blessings *(berachot)* there is a basic principle of primary and secondary considerations (*eekar* and *tafel*). When two food items, for example, are simultaneously available to be eaten, the blessing of primary concern supercedes the blessing of secondary concern. The prime purpose of the Jew is to learn Torah. Everything else—including secular scholarship—is of secondary value to the Jewish character. As a result, a blessing performed on a Jew occurs only when he excels in his basic, primary task—the study of Torah.

The Rosh HaYeshivah had many talents. His ethical lectures were masterpieces of precise system and logic. His ability to interpret the commentaries of the Maharal of Prague were in the realm of sheer genius. He was the Shakespeare of the Rosh HaYeshivas. His Torah knowledge and brilliant mind were acclaimed by the Torah sages of previous generations. He was the spiritual guide to the day school movement in America. He was a major voice in all great decisions affecting the world Torah community. All these items and more would require volumes to properly articulate and suitably comprehend. Yet to me, a former *talmid*, he was basically a *rebbe*. A Rosh HaYeshivah who excelled in his basic role. To me—and to countless others—that was his primary role. It is that role that requires a special *berachah* for it is that function that, to me, defines the essence of his genius.

Moreinu v'Rabbeinu = *Our master and our Teacher.*
Z.L. = *Zichrono Livrachah* = *May his memory be a blessing.*

59. Halachic Parameters of Truth

Society cherishes the virtue of truth as a cardinal precept of morality. It is the glue that cements relationships and permits the web of social interaction to exist.

Truth is so sanctified by moral suasion that its violation evokes stringent legal and societal punitive actions. No one wants an acknowledged liar as a leader, partner, business associate, mate, or friend. Most people believe, moreover, as Chaucer noted, that "truth will out." The truth is always eventually uncovered. Thus, both positive and negative sanctions serve as a deterrent to falsehood.

But life experiences are not always patterned on the basis of truth. Numerous occasions occur wherein the whole truth is either simply not told or is even withheld. Also, what about the phenomenon of the so-called white lie? Is a white lie an immoral act? Is it immoral to give false praise? If an individual inquires about our health, generally our response would be "fine" even though we may be racked with pain. Is such a response to be equated with lying?

Basic to the issue is the problem of whether the sanctity of truth possesses certain qualifications. Is it necessary for truth (the whole truth) to be told even though an adverse reaction may occur, e.g., hurting feelings, ruining reputations, and stimulating economic and/or political ramifications?

In addition, the issue has moral overtones relating to such fundamental concerns as whether it is proper to inform a dying person of the terminal nature of an illness. Since traditional

Judaism sanctifies social morality as a religious pursuit to the same extent as ritual observance, a halachic analysis, rather than a pure philosophical inquiry, must be developed.

The Talmud (*Shevuot* 31a) presents two interesting cases which may serve as the basis of an inquiry concerning the parameters of truth.

A. How do we know that a disciple sitting before his master, who sees that the poor man is right and the wealthy man wrong, should not remain silent? Because it is said: "From a false matter keep far" (Exodus 23:7).

B. A disciple to whom his master says, "You know that if I were given a hundred manehs, I would not tell a lie; now so-and-so owes me one maneh . . . [and] I have definitely one witness; you come and stand there, but you need not say anything, so that you will not be uttering a lie from your mouth;—(but the debtor will think you have come to give evidence and will perhaps admit the debt of his own accord). Even so, this is prohibited because it is said: "From a false matter keep far."

Case A teaches us that silence itself may be a form of falsehood. In a circumstance wherein silence would result in a definite erroneous legal decision, it is incumbent to speak out and rectify the wrong. Even though a case is being judged by the master rather than the disciple, and normally it would be considered audacious to contradict one's teacher, still the biblical injunction obligates one to reveal the truth. Personal qualms about ruffling the dignity of the master by contradicting his sagacity have no bearing on the issue.

Case B informs us that the illusion of falsehood is also falsehood. The case relates to a circumstance wherein moral questions pertain only to the process rather than the end result. The man may, indeed, owe the money to the master. But Jewish law requires a minimum of two witnesses to obligate repayment by court procedures. Thus, even though the debtor may be lying, it is still prohibited to provide an illusion of two witnesses in order to stimulate confession and repayment.

Had the Talmud, moreover, listed either of the cases, rather than both, it would have been difficult to generalize from one to the other. If the Talmud cited only Case A, it would have been possible to infer that silence is blameworthy only when a wrong result would occur. Therefore, it may be permitted to stand with a reliable witness to coerce a debtor to admit the truth. On the other hand, if the Talmud presented only Case B, it would be possible to assume that silence is prohibited as a form of falsehood only when it is accompanied by a positive activity, such as joining another witness. However, silent inaction may not be construed to be wrong.

Further insight may be gleaned from R. Hananel's comment that the above cases are instances of rabbinical allusions to Scripture. This comment suggests that these cases would not be proscribed by biblical law. They are, rather, rabbinical dictates based upon an interpretation of the scriptural mandate. The distinction between the biblical and rabbinical orientations is made on the basis of the translation of the scriptural Hebrew text, *Midvar sheker tirhak*. The term *dvar* may denote a spoken word or statement. A translation based upon the denotative meaning of the text would read: "From a false word, keep far." This means, perhaps, that Scripture proscribes only false statements—not silence. Utilizing the connotation of the term *dvar*, which means "matter" or "things," the rabbis extended the scope of the biblical statement. Accordingly, any activity—even silence—which brings about falsehood must be prohibited.

In addition, the rabbinical orientation may have focused upon a consideration of the distinct implication of the scriptural verse. The Bible does not proscribe telling a lie; rather, it suggests the desirability of maintaining a social and moral distance from falsehood.

No generalization should be made on the basis of the above citations because other talmudic sources suggest various different nuances concerning the parameters of truth. It is necessary to analyze each talmudic source before drawing any conclusions.

The Talmud in *Ketubot* 16b–17a notes:

> Our rabbis taught: "How does one dance before the bride?" Bait Shammai say: "The bride as she is." And Bait Hillel say: "Beautiful and graceful bride!" Bait Shammai said to Bait Hillel: "If she was lame or blind, does one say of her: 'Beautiful and graceful bride,' whereas the Torah said, 'Keep far from a false matter'?" Said Bait Hillel to Bait Shammai: "According to your word, if one had made a bad purchase in the market, should one praise it in his eyes or deprecate it? Surely, one should praise it in his eyes." Therefore, the sages said: "Always should the disposition of man be pleasant with people."

The sages were primarily concerned with the propriety of a wedding celebration rather than the form of a dance, so that they were intent upon formulating the wording of a greeting. There are several interpretations to this debate between Bait Shammai and Bait Hillel which shed light on the social dimensions of truth.

1. The Tosafot contend that in a case of a bride with a blemish, Bait Shammai's position is that one may either be silent or may elect to praise a particular physical attribute of beauty, such as the bride's eyes. Bait Hillel's position is that such selective praise implies other negative physical aspects. Thus, Bait Shammai does not establish a set phrase. The prohibition against involvement with falsehood necessitates that each bride be judged upon her own traits. Indeed, the value of truth is so vital that it overcomes any negative consideration or personal anguish that may result. On the other hand, Bait Hillel is concerned with the personal sentiments of

the bride. Every bride, regardless of any shortcomings, must be praised.

Bait Hillel's statement "Beautiful and graceful bride" is not considered a falsehood in the case of a bride with blemishes, for the phrase may relate to the bride's actions (character), not her physical traits (see *Korban Netanel*). The debate may, therefore, be about the type of falsehood prohibited by Scripture. Bait Shammai would contend that falsehood relates to the denotation of the word or phrase uttered. If common parlance gives a specific meaning to a phrase, and facts appear to vitiate such usage in a particular situation, then no matter what connotative meanings are intended, such a phrase would be unacceptable. Since beauty generally relates to physical traits rather than to character, this quality should not be applied to one who lacks physical beauty. Bait Hillel maintains that falsehood is prohibited only when even a connotation of truth is missing. Thus, the term "beauty" may be applied to one lacking physical beauty because, in this particular case, it may be said to relate to her character. As a result, it is not prohibited.

This may have been the motivation behind the forced explanation in Genesis 20:11–12 as to why Abraham stated that Sarah was his sister rather than his wife. Sarah was supposedly his sister since she was the daughter of his father but not of his mother. Commentaries, moreover, state that in ancient times a niece was called a daughter and a female cousin was called a sister. According to Bait Hillel's interpretation, as long as a connotative meaning may be applied to a term it is not regarded as a reprehensible falsehood.

Indeed, the story in Genesis further refines the parameters of truth. Abraham is defended for calling Sarah his sister because of two motives: (1) he was fearful for his life; (2) Sarah was, indeed, called his sister. Why were both reasons presented? Is not a person permitted to lie in order to save his life? On the one hand, why was it even necessary to suggest that the action was not a falsehood? Also, if a connotative meaning is applicable, why was it necessary to suggest that Abraham's life was in danger?

It may be suggested that moral dilemmas do not necessarily relate to problems of good and bad or right and wrong. Rather, moral problems may relate to decisions between right and right and good and good. It is rare that a person may be in a quandary when the line of demarcation between right and wrong is clear. It is right to tell the truth. It is also right to save one's life. When two positive values may be in conflict with each other, one must determine the relative importance of each, the impact or consequence of such a choice, and the conditions under which one of the values may be violated. It is obvious that saving one's life is more vital than uttering a true statement. Yet, to righteous Abraham, it was preferable to act in a fashion that did not appear to involve him in a falsehood.

Truth, in general cases, relates to the denotation of the term expressed. When, for example, the value of truth is in conflict with another value of greater importance, then, as long as the connotative meaning is utilized, no evidence of falsehood may be considered. Thus, when the feelings of a bride may be hurt and family harmony may be jeopardized, one may extend truth to mean connotative interpretations. Bait Shammai, however, would contend that the anguish of the bride is not sufficiently important to permit a "loose" interpretation of the prohibition against a falsehood.

2. The *Taz* (R. David b. Shemuel Halevi, 1586–1667, Russia, Poland) and the *Maharsha* (R. Shemuel Eliezer Halevi Aydels, 1555–1631, Poland, Austria) present an alternative position concerning the debate between Bait Shammai and Bait Hillel (*Ketubot* 17a, *Even Ha-ezer* 65:1). They contend that Bait Shammai was as concerned as Bait Hillel with developing a universally applicable ritual phrase. Accordingly, the term "the bride as she is" was to be recited. The motivation for this interpretation is that to praise beautiful brides while providing limited

accolades to others is an act of public humiliation that no one should condone. To fulfill the requirement of keeping far from falsehood, an innocuous statement was to be used. It simply meant that the bride appears as, indeed, a bride should. Bait Hillel, however, contends that the grace and beauty of the bride should be noted regardless of her actual physical traits. The reason is that at least in the eyes of the bridegroom the bride has beauty and grace. Bait Hillel, therefore, presents substantiation from a case of a purchase wherein it is common practice to assume that the purchaser desired that which was purchased.

According to Bait Shammai, statements are to be judged on the basis of universal application. If a bride is generally considered not to be beautiful, it is wrong to praise her beauty, even though her bridegroom may rave about her physical traits. Truth, therefore, according to Bait Shammai, does not relate to social and personal situations but rather is a universal moral concept. Bait Hillel, however, contends that the morality of statements is closely intertwined with social considerations. To the extent that beauty and grace are relative terms—so, too, is the morality (truth or falsehood) of such statements. Thus, in a situation wherein it is assumed that at least one person in the case considers the phrase truthful, no moral condemnation may be manifested.

3. The *Rashash* (R. Shemuel Shtarshon, Wilno, Poland) presents a third position relating to truth and falsity. He is concerned with two specific phrases of the text in *Ketubot*. In response to Bait Shammai's concern that a statement praising the beauty of an unbeautiful person may be morally incorrect, Bait Hillel said, "According to your words, if one had made a bad purchase in the market, should one praise it . . . or deprecate it?"

Two questions may therefore be asked of Bait Hillel.

1. What is the meaning of the term "according to your words"? Also, why was the term "market" utilized rather than the term "merchant"? The *Rashash* theorizes that it is a mitzvah

to tell the truth and, therefore, incumbent upon a person to advise a friend of a bad purchase made from a known merchant. In a situation, however, where a purchase was made at a market wherein the seller is not known, then, and only then, is it wrong to cause personal anguish by defaming a purchase which cannot be returned. Thus, it is not reprehensible to present praise wherein no practical result would occur by telling the truth. For example, Bait Shammai is of the opinion that, once married, divorce can only be granted in instances of adultery, since there is now no practical moral mode of dissolving the marriage. Bait Hillel said, "According to you . . . [Bait Shammai], there is no basic benefit in telling the truth concerning the appearance of the bride."

This theory presents a standard with which to judge moral statements. If truth will rectify an error, then it is incumbent to tell the truth. If, however, no remedy exists to correct a problem, then it is moral to present praise, even if it is not necessarily the truth. The Halachah is according to Bait Hillel (*Even Ha-ezer* 65:1).

All the arguments presented suggest that there is no obligation to reveal the truth in all circumstances. For instance, a person is not obligated to inform an ugly person in the street that he (or she) is ugly. The reason, we can deduce, is that Scripture does not state, "Truth must be told." Instead, the Bible merely inhibits a falsehood from being uttered.

The three theories may now be related to the talmudic text in *Shevuot* wherein it was noted that silence is a form of falsehood. According to the position of the Tosafot, a connotation of truth is sufficient to judge a statement as moral if the dilemma is between the value of telling the truth and the value of not hurting the feelings of others. In the case of *Shevuot*, however, another ingredient is injected, i.e., deceitfully extracting money from a person. Under such a circumstance, the truth must be revealed.

Both the *Maharsha* and the *Taz* suggest that statements which appear on the surface to be untruthful may not actually be reprehensible in cases delineating a situation in which the purchaser of an article is assumed to comprehend fully the terms and conditions of his purchase. However, where no prior understanding of right and wrong or truth and falsity are listed, as is the case in *Shevuot*, then even silence is prohibited.

The *Rashash* contends that truth must be revealed whenever it may rectify a situation. Therefore, it is logical that silence is immoral when it may create a wrong act or decision. From the above we conclude that in monetary cases the whole truth must be revealed.

Yet another interpretation of Bait Hillel's position vastly expands the moral dimensions of truth. The *Ritvah* (R. Yomtov b. Avraham [Ashbeelee], d. 1342, Spain) suggests that Bait Hillel permits all brides to be lauded as being beautiful, for truth may generally be modified for purposes of shalom (peace).

This general rule is cited in *Yevamot* 65b as follows:

1. R. Elai said in the name of R. Elazar b. Shamua: It is permitted for a man to modify [a report] in the interest of peace, as it is said [Gen. 50:16], "Thy father did command [etc.], so shall ye say unto Joseph: O forgive, I pray thee."
2. R. Jonathan says, It is a religious duty [to modify], as it is said [I Sam. 16:2], "and Samuel said: How shall I go? If Saul should hear it, he would kill me," etc.
3. At the college of R. Ishmael it was taught: Peace is a great thing, for even the Holy One, praised be He, modified [Sarah's words] for her sake, as the verse says in the beginning [Gen. 18:12], "and my master [Abraham] is old," and afterwards it is said, "and I am old."

(Elaborations of these texts may be noted in the Midrash. See, for example, *Lev. Rabbah*, chap. 9.)

The first case relates to the fear of Joseph's brothers that

Joseph would punish them for their misdeeds against him after Jacob, their father, had died. They, therefore, informed Joseph that prior to his death, Jacob had made a specific command to implore Joseph to forgive the sins of his brothers. Yet nowhere in Scripture is any reference made to such a command by Jacob prior to his death. As a result, the Talmud derives the dictum that truth may be modified for purposes of family peace.

The second illustration is part of the story wherein Samuel was commanded to visit the house of Jesse to anoint a king to replace Saul. Samuel was fearful that King Saul would hear of such intentions and would murder him to retain his rule over Israel. To assuage such fears, the Almighty told Samuel to inform everyone that his purpose in the area was to offer certain sacrifices. He did not have to reveal the true purpose of his visit. Truth was modified to establish an aura of peace and harmony. It is, perhaps, called a mitzvah in this case since the Almighty Himself suggested the subterfuge.

The third citation refers to an act of withholding information for purposes of family harmony. In Genesis, when Sarah was first informed by a divine messenger that she would give birth, she presented two negative reactions: (1) she was too old to bear a child; (2) Abraham, her husband, was too old. Thus, the advanced ages of both mates were noted as mitigating factors against the birth of a child. Yet, when Sarah's response was related to Abraham, the Almighty informed him only of Sarah's contention of her advanced age and not of her statement that Abraham was too old to father a child. The negative information was withheld so as not to cause anguish to Abraham.

The halachic orientation, therefore, is that in a conflict between telling the truth and disrupting family harmony or personal peace, the moral value of truth is secondary to the moral value of peace. This general rule seems to conflict with the textual arguments presented in the citations relating to the debate between Bait Shammai and Bait Hillel. If the Halachah is that truth may be altered for the purpose of peace, then why did not Bait Hillel state this law to substantiate its viewpoint rather than provide support for its position by citing an anecdote of a person making a purchase? A simple retort to Bait Shammai could have been that the scriptural mandate against falsehood is not applicable in cases where truth is altered to preserve family peace or tranquility.

The Sephardic author of *Ben Yohoyada* suggests (*Yevamot* 65b) that the general rule permitting truth to be altered for purposes of peace has a basic limitation: i.e., the rule relates only to a situation where there is a preexisting problem where an untrue statement may maintain calm and harmony. However, where no prior problematic condition exists, the general rule is not applicable and additional reasons must be developed to sustain any alteration of truth.

The three scriptural references cited above support *Ben Yohoyada*'s theory. Joseph had, indeed, suffered as a result of the actions of his brothers. King Saul, moreover, was known to jealously guard his royal image and the regal trappings of his office. A modification of truth was, therefore, permitted in both cases to assuage feelings. In the case of Abraham and Sarah, it was indeed a fact that Sarah had questioned the virility of Abraham. The retelling of such a fact could only serve to hurt Abraham's pride. As a result, Sarah's statement was simply not mentioned.

In the case of an unbeautiful bride, however, there is no known, preexisting statement of a derogatory or unkind nature. On the contrary, the woman is being married, and ostensibly no one has made any negative statement. Thus, Bait Hillel found it necessary to develop a unique motivation for the altering of truth. To advance its argument, Bait Hillel introduced the anecdote of the purchases. Once Bait Hillel developed a reason for declaring all brides beautiful, the end result was that this case could also now be applied to the general rule; namely, that truth may be altered for the purpose of peace. This may be the explanation of the *Ritvah's* position.

Another possible distinction between the citations is that the Talmud in *Yevamot* relates only to circumstances where the altering of the truth does not contradict known facts. Then it may be permitted either to add a statement or to withhold information. However, to say that an ugly person is beautiful requires a special explanation. It is for this reason that Bait Hillel does not substantiate its theory by citing the general rule noted in *Yevamot*.

Indeed, the rule that truth may be altered for purposes of peace (with the above-noted limitations) is quite distinct from the cases relating to monetary circumstances noted by the Talmud in *Shevuot*. A decision in a monetary case may bring tranquility to one party and anguish to another. Therefore, the altering of the truth, even by silence, cannot be condoned. No true peace may result.

Basic to a comprehensive understanding of the talmudic notion that truth may be altered for purposes of peace is an apparent contradiction noted in yet another talmudic citation. The Talmud (*Yevamot* 63a) states:

Rav's wife caused him anguish. When he asked her to prepare for him lentils, she would prepare small peas for him; and when he asked for peas, she would prepare lentils. When his son Hiya grew up, he used to reverse [the orders, and thus the result was just what Rav wanted]. "Thy mother improved herself," Rav once remarked to his son. To which his son replied: "I caused it, because I reversed the orders." Whereupon Rav said to him: "This is what people say: 'Thy own descendant will teach thee sense.' However, thou shalt not do so [anymore], because it is said [Jer. 9:4], 'They have taught their tongue to speak falsehood, they weary themselves to commit iniquity.' "

Since Hiya had altered the truth to bring honor to his father and peace to his home, should not such acts have been praised, rather than prohibited?

The *Rashal* (R. Solomon Luria, 1510–1573, Poland) suggests that habitual altering of the truth (as in the case of Hiya to his mother) is to be condemned as repugnant to the development of character even though the purpose is to promote family tranquility (see also *Maharsha*). The modification of truth for purposes of peace is permitted only on an occasional, infrequent basis. Thus, even the positive value of peace cannot always be utilized to sanction white lies.

The *Iyun Yaakov* (R. Jacob b. Joseph Reicher—Jacob Back, d. 1733, Austria), in a commentary on the *Ein Yaakov,* contends that the truth may not be modified for purposes of peace when the true nature of the issue can easily and subsequently be revealed. Since Rav might personally request his food rather than utilize his son, the trick might be discovered and complications could result. This means that a white lie is permitted for purposes of family peace only in such circumstances that it would forever remain a secret.

The guidelines presented herein underscore the moral considerations of acts of speech. Any oral statement is a process of revealing and withholding information, for it reflects a conscious and subconscious determination of what to say, how to say it, and how much to say. Coupled with this is the dilemma of whether it is proper even to make a statement at all. As a result of this process of moral judgments, a scintilla of error may be present even in a statement generally accepted as truth. This factor may be the motivation impelling some pious Jews to refrain from taking an oath even on matters known to be truthful.

The Midrash relates that synagogues in Jerusalem were destroyed because individuals made truthful oaths. It is for this reason, perhaps, that in *Pirkei Avot* it states: "All my life I have dwelt among scholars, and never have I found anything better than silence" (see *Midrash Tanhuma,* Leviticus, also *Midrash Rabbah,* Numbers).

Indeed, the Jewish orientation toward truth indicates a

unique positive dimension. Georg Simmel, the German sociologist, for example, contends that a lie contains two dysfunctional elements: (1) it is an erroneous statement of fact; and (2) it withholds from the recipient the true sentiment of the speaker. As a result, untruth creates a social distance between two people. Therefore, to bridge the gap of social distance, truthful knowledge of the concerns of a fellow person is essential.

Jewish tradition similarly intertwines love and knowledge in interpersonal relations. Scripture has a phrase in which the Almighty notes of Abraham (Genesis 18:19): "I know him." Rahsi interprets this to mean, "I love him." Rashi's explanation is that love and knowledge are closely intertwined. The more one loves a person, the more one seeks to have knowledge of him. Yet this does not mean that the withholding of information is an act of stifling or lowering the intensity of love. The Jewish tradition considers the withholding of information at times a positive, functional act necessitated by the dictates of love and compassion. Total truth may be an act of estrangement, and a white lie may be an act of love. The morality of statements must not be viewed in abstract terms but, rather, in terms of specific situational factors.

On the basis of the sources cited above, it can be deduced that there is no general rule relating to the morality of truth, since it is not always moral to tell the truth, and it may, indeed, be moral to tell a white lie or to remain silent. Therefore, in each circumstance, one must determine which viewpoint is applicable.

Caveat: The above presentation in no way attempts to provide definitive halachic-talmudic solutions to the moral dilemma. Rather, it seeks to stimulate further thought, analysis, and discussion within the context of Judaism's traditional concern for strengthening ethics and morality.

60. Why Fight for Civil Rights: A Dialogue (1963)

AARON: Saul! Hello! What brings you down here to the South?

SAUL: Well if it isn't . . . Aaron, hi! It's good to see you again. I've just come with a group of fellows from up North to help out the Negroes with this vicious racial problem they're having. . . . Hey, why the smile? Don't tell me you're on the other side? Don't you think fighting for civil equality is important?

AARON: I'm sorry, I . . . I didn't mean to dampen your enthusiasm or even imply that it's not an important cause. In fact, it's one of the most important issues of our time. But, it just appears peculiar that you should be one of the people to come. It simply doesn't fit your character at all.

SAUL: Come now, Aaron, what sort of talk is that? What do you mean?

AARON: Well, we've been good friends for a long time. I know you pretty well. I remember the long, intense discussions we've had together. Yes, I recall how you continually attempted to portray religion as a meaningless area of concern with no practical content for our modern age. Those were your beliefs, and you as an individual had a right to hold them. But what appears incongruous is that a nonbeliever in religion should serve as an aggressive champion of Negro rights.

SAUL: This argument of yours is a real solid one, that is, for a man living in the fourteenth or fifteenth century. What kind of reasoning are you trying to pull on me? Are you maintaining that one who is not religious has no right to subscribe to or campaign for basic moral issues? Why, that whole concept went out of style a long time ago. One belief has nothing to do with the other. I'm downright surprised that a modern, educated person like you could ever make such an erroneous assumption.

AARON: I see you haven't lost your skill of debate. You're still adept at turning defensive positions into offensive ones. But I'm serious and not interested in having a mere mental exercise with you. I realize that my previous words may appear strange and outdated. Yet I know (mind you, I'm saying that I know, not I feel, not I think, but I know) that from a rational and logical point of view it is inconceivable that a negator of religion should fight for minority rights. The reason people consider such a view to be antiquated is simply because they never seriously think about it. Now, since you're so intent upon helping resolve the racial problem and have traveled so many miles to accomplish this feat, I think you should be quite clear as to what you are doing before you rush headfirst into this delicate matter. So, let's discuss the basic issues. Perhaps we'll find out who is right and who is wrong.

SAUL: I see you are serious, and I would like to know what's on your mind, so, O.K., let's talk. Let's discuss the entire matter. Though I doubt it, perhaps something interesting will result.

AARON:Let's start at the beginning. First of all, I believe that for many reasons a terrible crime is being committed against the Negroes. But my views should be of no concern to you at present. The crucial present problem is—why are *you* so incensed about the way the Negroes are treated in the South? What's wrong with it?

SAUL: Aha, so that's your game. For argument's sake you want to take the role of the Southern white. Fine, that's O.K. with me. I'll tell you what irked me and why I came. It is my feeling that racial discrimination is a flagrant violation of all codes of ethics and morality. You know what's going on down here. Why, no ethical person could be quiet when such brutality exists. Indeed, the morality of our nation is at stake if we allow people to be crudely deprived of their basic rights.

AARON: This is a *really* altruistic answer. Had you said that the Constitution of the United States as well as the decisions of the Supreme Court are being violated, then I could understand your role quite clearly. You would have been an indignant citizen seeking to ensure that the laws of our country are being obeyed. But that is not your argument. You're too sophisticated for such a claim. You'd rather portray yourself as the embodiment of morality, the spokesman for ethical conduct. What right have you to do that? What right have you to put yourself on a pedestal and look down upon the ethical conduct of others? How do you even know that the Southern treatment of the Negro is unethical? What's your guide? What's your standard for ethics?

SAUL: My standard? You ask for my personal standard of ethics? Why, I speak in the name of universal ethics. The idea that all men have an inalienable right to be treated decently. No, no, this is not a standard that I dreamed up. This is the standard of humanity; the guide of all decent men.

AARON: This is no answer. You merely state that the standard you use is not yours but that of some dubious group called humanity. Who made up this universal ethic? Which group of people had the audacity to make up a code by which all nations, all people may be judged? Secondly, who ever said there's a code of morality by which all may be guided?

SAUL: I'll deal with your second question first. Yes, there is a universal ethic. There is a guide of morality overseeing all people. The proof of this is that we condemn the Nazis for tormenting, torturing, and killing Jews. This is not a theory. This is a basic fact. And had there been no universal ethic, this would be impossible. But, since we do condemn the Germans, we ipso facto recognize that all nations must abide by a universal ethic. Now, who created this code? Why, it's society. Not mine alone, but the society of mankind. This is the group that made the ethics for all to follow.

AARON: In other words, society creates ethics. Is this correct?

SAUL: Yes. Society as a whole establishes morality.

AARON: This, my friend, is a most tenuous position to defend. If this be the case, I say we haven't any rational right to condemn the Germans for brutally killing Jews. If society has the right to establish morality, then any code they create becomes, by definition, moral. It therefore follows that he who goes against society is unethical. Under such a situation during the Nazi regime, wherein it was decided by that society that Jews are harmful creatures and that a good Nazi citizen must destroy them, it, again by definition, made such acts "moral." Indeed, the German who was sympathetic to Jews is actually, in those terms, "immoral."

SAUL: Wait a minute, Aaron, slow down. You're jumping to conclusions. I said society as a whole, including all of mankind, creates ethics. Not one individual nation or group.

AARON: True, that is what you said. But you also must know that each society establishes laws and mores for its own national interest. Each society assumes that its laws are correct. Now, Nazi Germany believed it was ethical to kill Jews; ancient Spartans considered it moral to rid themselves of aged people not productive to society; certain cultures felt it correct to destroy young girls when they believed that their society had sufficient numbers of them; Communist Russia, in the interest of the state, massacred millions of people. These groups certainly believed they were correct. Can we condemn them?

SAUL: Certainly.

AARON: How? What right have we to impose our ethics upon them? How do we know that the moral code of the United States is correct and applicable for all nations? Maybe the Spartan, Communist, or Nazi system is correct. If society creates ethics, the problem always revolves around the pivotal question of whether one society has the right to assume that its code of ethics is universally to be accepted. The Communists believe they are right. We believe our way is best. Yet what right have we to say that our code should be the standard for the entire world? Every culture has the right to create a code to best satisfy its own selfish national interest. And every society should have the right to negate any standard which in its collective mind is detrimental to its perception of national safety. Basically the question is, how can we condemn a society for following its own conception of morality? How do we know that our way of life is best for all?

SAUL: I see age has sharpened your logic. But there is a good answer to your problem. It is that all moral law is based upon a consensus of opinion of rational men. Look at the world; all rational, decent people condemn torture and cruelty. This consensus of opinion of men and women throughout the world establishes the code to judge all nations.

AARON: I thought that you would come up with a better answer than that. It appears that you are implying that we count the decent people of the world and see what minimum ethical rules they have. And then, this becomes the guide for humanity. This, my friend, is a fallacious contention. Allow me to explain why. There are two forms of theories. One is a factual theory, and the other a normative one. A factual theory is exactly what it states. It is a theory that relates to a question of facts. For example, should one have a theory that there are 220 million people in the United States today, this theory may be shown to be correct or incorrect by amassing certain factual data. If, as a result of counting the people, the facts show that there are 220 million people, then my theory is correct. If, on the other hand, facts show that there are less than this sum, then my theory is incorrect.

SAUL: Of course, a factual theory is one that may be verified by resorting to factual data.

AARON: Right. Now a normative theory is one that relates to

questions concerning how one *ought* to act, rather than how people actually do behave. Democracy, communism, and Judaism are all normative theories. They are theories telling people how they ought to behave. One certainly cannot state that the theories of Judaism are incorrect merely because a census was made showing that people do not completely observe the dictates of these theories. One can't say that democracy is worthless because American people don't fully practice democratic precepts. Indeed, all normative theories are by definition things not necessarily found in reality. They are ideas, principles holding forth patterns of behavior and goals to work for. They don't describe the way people are, but, rather, outline the way they should be. Now, with this understood, one simply couldn't determine the correctness of any ethical code by resorting to a consensus of opinion. One can't say that if the majority of people believe that it is correct to kill and plunder, cheat and deceive, that these things are right and, therefore, should become the standard morality for all. Isn't it probable that the majority may be wrong? This is the crucial problem. We can't logically establish a universal ethic by resorting to factual data or a consensus of opinion, as just shown, and at the same time, we do, at least, emotionally and psychologically feel that the Nazi and Spartan systems of ethics should be condemned. But maybe they shouldn't? Why doesn't each society have the right to do what they want to? And if this point be granted, then it would appear almost impossible to construct a universal ethic. For any code established would always be open to suspicion. It may always be challenged by saying that it is good for the nation or society that created it, but not for any other. The question of personal national interest or orientation may be leveled at any moral guide.

SAUL: I see the problem. Yes, you're right. I hadn't really thought of this approach. I admit, I . . . I can't answer you. In fact, I even see what you're leading up to. You're trying to make me realize that from an ethical point of view the South-

ern whites have the right to treat the Negroes the way they
want to. Yes, now I understand your distinction between a
constitutional approach and an ethical one. From the stand-
point of constitutional law, the Negroes must get a fair deal.
This is the law, and all, North and South, must comply with it.
But from a moral point of view, the absence of a universal ethic
presents each culture with the right to construct its own moral
guide. The Southern society, therefore, has the right to formu-
late any system they want, and other groups have no justification to morally condemn them. Yes, the more I think about it
the more plausible it appears. Just as the Communists establish
their peculiar brand of justice and morality, so too have societal
groups, no matter how large or small, the right to create their
own ethical patterns. But why did you interweave the concept
of religion into this matter? Why should a religious person
have the right to champion ethical values? What distinction is
there between the unreligious and the religious person?

AARON: You're right. I was going to lead up to the situation
in the South, and your logical conclusion is basically the one I
wanted to present. Now, concerning your question, I do
believe that there is a vast distinction between the nonbeliever
and the religious person concerning ethical judgments. Since,
as we previously saw, no society or cluster of societies has the
right to assume that its code must be accepted by all, the
problem always remains as to the criteria for judging or condemning a society with an orientation different from ours. But
we do, as you correctly said, condemn the actions of other
groups. This implies that we, at least, psychologically assume
that there is a universal standard of conduct. What is it? Is our
assumption correct? As long as society is the guide for ethics,
then our assumption is completely fallacious. But if ethics were
created by something independent of society, independent of a
selfish national interest, then it would be logically possible to
have a universal code of morality. It would basically be a code
that transcends all nations.

SAUL: Well, whatever this "something" is, it certainly can't be human. For any individual or societal group, no matter how large, according to your logic is open to the charge of self-interest or personal ethics. So what could this "something" be?

AARON: You're so right. This "something" certainly can't be human. It must be free from all human faults and prejudices. In fact, there's only one thing that fits this description: God.

SAUL: God? How did you get Him in here?

AARON: Well, the only thing I can conceive of that has no limitations, that has no human frailties, is God. Only a God can construct a code applicable to all. Only God, who is the Creator of all mankind, has the right to judge all cultures. Think about it. With God as the criterion for morality, do we still have the objections raised before? Certainly not. To the extent that He is not just the God of America or Africa, but of the entire world, one cannot raise the question of national interest. Indeed, only a religious person who believes in a God who gave mankind a code, such as we Jews believe happened on Sinai, can judge humanity from an ethical point of view. We can say that the Nazis, Spartans, Communists, and Southerners are wrong because they violate the divine code of morality—a code that supersedes all patterns of behavior, for it comes from God and is therefore absolute justice applicable to all. We can say that no society has the moral right to deprive an individual of his rights. And we can base our statements on the law of God that transcends all societal boundaries. Should one negate the validity of a God-given law, then one casts off all claims to a universal code of morality. In such a case anything goes. Now you must admit that religion, according to our arguments, is of great importance. It is not just an abstract system of concepts for the pious or meek. No, far from it. Religion is a very practical and basic area of concern. It gives mankind a basis for morality and a standard for action.

SAUL: You're getting to me, Aaron, but I still don't think you've presented a clear total picture of the matter. You're saying that if one accepts religion with its concept of a God-given code, then one has a valid standard for judging the actions of others. Yet the opposite is not necessarily true. According to your theory, if one doesn't believe in God, then one has no standard for morality, and life is simply chaotic. But this may be shown to be false. Look at all the people who don't accept the dictates of religion. Why, look at such men as Bertrand Russell, the philosopher. He doesn't believe in God, yet he's quite ethical. In fact, he's just one of the countless people who do not believe in God and are extremely ethical in all their actions.

AARON: I expected that question from you long ago, and I believe it was already answered when we saw that if one doesn't believe in a *Torah M'Sinai,* God-given law, then each group or individual is free to compose his own brand of ethics. It may happen that a multitude of people will come to the conclusion, for numerous reasons, that it is wrong to kill, torture, steal, and cheat. But at the same time it's quite possible that another group may establish a code exceedingly different from the one we normally consider to be ethical, and neither has a rational right to impose its standards upon the other. Thus, an individual may be supposedly ethical in his conduct without religion, but he has no justification to judge others. This means that without God all matters pertaining to ethics are personal and have no universal validity.

SAUL: In other words, we need God so that we can condemn people. Isn't that a peculiar statement to make?

AARON: I didn't say that. You're twisting my words.

SAUL: Yes, you did. You said that only a religious person has the right to condemn others, for he has the God-given standard for morality. It, therefore, appears that if you didn't have God around, no one would be able to denounce or condemn another. Wouldn't that be a better world?

AARON: My, this is a switch. Weren't you so intent about condemning the Southern community a little while ago? How did you now become so pacific?

SAUL: It's not a question of pacifism. I just want a clarification of your ideas, for it seems strange that the goal of religion should be portrayed as the only code upon which one may condemn people.

AARON: The goal of religion is not to condemn people, but, rather, to establish order in the world. It gives us a guide for praise as well as for blame. It shows what we can or cannot do. In fact, there's more need for such a code today than at any other time. The social distance of the world is shrinking. What happens in Africa or Asia has practical ramifications in the United States. No nation or societal group stands alone. We're all intertwined in the fine fabric of a close-knit general society. In this situation, more than ever before we need a universal ethic. We need to know how to judge actions—those of our own and those of others. We just can't vegetate or scramble wildly to the moon. We need a code to tell us what to do and what we may aspire to attain. This is religion; this is Torah; this is its practical need for our modern age. This gives us the moral justification to fight for minority rights, this and nothing else.

SAUL: In other words, my cause is just, but my reasons for it are not.

AARON: Exactly. Maybe . . .

SAUL: I must interrupt you. My train is leaving. I do wish I had more time to talk with you. But I'll consider what you said. I'll think about it. Somehow I still believe that ethics has nothing to do with religion. There are still several things I would like cleared up. But your arguments are quite good. I don't know. I don't know.

AARON: So long, my friend. At least one thing I have proved.

SAUL: What's that?

AARON: That you have to think about religion. That you just can't push it aside as a meaningless area of concern. That religion, that Torah, may be the only vehicle for the establishment of a universal ethic.

SAUL: Yes, there is something to it. You have to think about it. Perhaps you're right about the whole thing. Yes, you may be right.

61. *Agnon's Yom Kippur Symbol*

The selection but a few years ago of Shmuel Yosef Agnon, as a recipient of the Nobel Prize for Literature generated a qualitatively different degree of Jewish pride than the type evinced when other Jewish scholars and scientists were so acclaimed. When a person estranged from his religious heritage wins an international award in a discipline not related to Judaism, it serves as but another fine example of the reoccurring genius of the Jew; a popular manifestation of the fervent will to achieve and ability to succeed that has marked the historicity of the Jewish nation. When, however, the laurels of the Nobel Prize were presented to a man such as Agnon, a committed, observant Jew, for his talented artistry in dramatically recreating Jewish life, culture, and tradition, then it was not merely the genius of the Jew that was acclaimed but also the glory of our heritage itself.

Agnon was not an analyst of modern Jewish life or activity. His role may be conceived as a spiritual historian of our people rather than a creator of fictional imagery and events. His inspirational message and artistry require a basic understanding of Jewish traditions and symbols before they may truly be understood or appreciated. This essay is an attempt to present a guideline to Agnon's writings by analyzing his usage of certain distinctive religious symbols.

A perusal of Agnon's works discloses a tendency to continually interweave some reference to Yom Kippur into the fine fabric of his stories. This tendency may be due to two factors.

One, the richness of the Yom Kippur symbol enables Agnon to enhance and fortify the images he desired to present. Two, this symbol may be intertwined with his own conception of life and his role as a writer.

But a few citations may support the former consideration. In the novel *Tmol Shilshom*, Agnon presents a brief sketch of Y. Kumar's fond memories of his pious mother. Here Kumar is described as one who occasionally remembers his mother as she appeared on Yom Kippur, dressed in white with her voice full of mercy.[1] By associating Kumar's mother with the symbol of Yom Kippur, Agnon is subtly clothing her in a garb of saintliness and religiosity. Thus the reverent feelings towards his mother receive added significance as a result of the use of this symbol.

In the novelette *Bilvav Yamin*, a major feature is the narration of the vicissitudes experienced by Hananyah, a poor yet righteous man, in his inspired endeavors to reach the Holy Land of Palestine. During his travail he accidently forgets the days of the week and thus transgresses the day of Yom Kippur.[2] In relating this episode of sin, Agnon provokes a deep emotional image. Yom Kippur is a Day of Atonement for error; a period wherein even those who forget or negate Judaism throughout the year flock to the synagogue to manifest some form of religiosity. The transgression is thus magnified by having it committed by a Godly man on a day proclaimed holy even by the irreligious; a transgression of such a nature that it is enacted in a period when all pray for forgiveness.

A third example may also be discerned within this story. While traveling through Europe, the pleasant, sad songs of the shepherd are heard and compared to a prayer on Yom Kippur.[3] This reference to Yom Kippur, to a people with hearts rent with hope for forgiveness, lifting up their voices in prayer of song, poignantly articulates the Jew's own experience with pleasant, sad songs.

While the above clearly show how the symbol of Yom Kippur

is used to stimulate in the minds of the readers a penetrating emotional image, it may also be shown that this symbol reflects a personal philosophical orientation of the writer.

This concept may be gleaned from the novel *Oreach Natah Lalun*. This is the story of Agnon's visit to Buczacz, the city of his birth and early youth. Arriving on the eve of Yom Kippur, he finds its despoiled condition to be markedly different from the beautiful images invoked by his dreams. On the following day, Yom Kippur, Agnon is told that many people are to leave this city of poverty and persecution and seek their fortune elsewhere. In addition, he is presented with the key to the old Beth HaMidrash, the place where once the voice of Torah echoed through its chambers. The place where Agnon as a youth delved into his studies and imaginatively dreamed of his future. This Beth HaMidrash is now devoid of Torah and dreams. It is empty, cold, and desolate. Yet Agnon fervently grasps and accepts its key. With this key he reopens its doors and with it reopens the history of his past. Numerous hours are spent learning in the Beth HaMidrash. In the winter he rekindles its fire and thus rekindles the old echo of Torah and prayer. For, as a result of the warmth of the fire in the Beth HaMidrash, many poverty-stricken Jews came in to warm their bodies and at the same time warm their soul with prayer and Torah.

As Agnon remains in Buczacz, he becomes involved with old and new friends whose biographical histories are related to him. As a result, within his mind can be found an integrated chronicle of the events of the town.

What does this story mean? What are its symbolic implications? It is our contention that the concept of Yom Kippur permeates this story and sheds light on its meaning.

Yom Kippur is the day of the year for atonement of sin. On this day one searches and analyzes the avenues of the past in order to prepare for the future. Forgiveness and a clear slate await those who are able to make peace with their past.

On the eve of Yom Kippur Agnon arrives in the city of his youth. A city known to him only in his dreams. Agnon possesses the spirit of Yom Kippur. He wants to know the past, not from dreams but from reality. He wants to inhale the invigorating breath of reality and perceive with his eyes and discern with his ears the true history of the past.

The setting for the confrontation of two opposing outlooks on life is found to be Buczacz, the city of destruction, and Yom Kippur, the day of righteous memories. On this day Agnon looks to the past, while the people look only to the future; Agnon wants to relive, and emotionally revive, the past; the people want no share of it. Agnon wants to stay in Buczacz, the people want to leave.

Is it not of symbolic importance that the key to the old Beth HaMidrash, which is actually the key to the intellectual and emotional treasures of his youth, is presented to him on Yom Kippur? It appears as if the mystical powers of this awe-inspiring day ordained him to be the custodian of its spirit and message. Yes, Agnon became the personification of Yom Kippur. His Yom Kippur message, to invoke and analyze the experiences of the past, is not only his goal as a writer but also his function as a man.

This novel relates that when Agnon met with most of the town's people, they began to retell the stories of the past. His information was gathered not in a mechanical fashion, but as one who thinks of his own experiences and by flashes of insight slowly begins to unfold an articulate story.

The recording of this story, as well as his other works, is the act of fulfilling his role as the living spirit of the Yom Kippur message. His stories retell the living experiences of Jews, whether in Israel or Europe. Lest we forget, his writings are here to remind us.

With this symbolic interpretation we may also discern the meaning of Agnon's short story "Im Kenisat Hayom." This is the story of a man who flees with his daughter the terrors of persecution and destruction. On the eve of Yom Kippur he arrives at the city of his youth. Entering the synagogue, which invokes fond memories of past wonderful experiences, his daughter's garment catches on fire and begins to burn. As a result she is left without any clothing. Having no garment to cover her, he goes to the home of an old friend to plead for help. This is of no avail, for they treat him as a stranger and speak only of their own needs. Returning to the synagogue he notices that people are beginning to come for the evening prayers. These people not only do not offer to help, but rather insult them or stare at their helplessness.

This story symbolizes the type of situation which Agnon desires to remedy. It is the story of people forgetting their obligation to remember. Here we see the evening of Yom Kippur, the entrance of a period which traditionally demands all to recall the past, failing to impress or dent the callousness of the people. Their crime in forgetting the bonds of friendship and kindness is significant in that it is committed on the day to recall.

Agnon perceives that people are forgetting their roots and old bonds. His uniqueness as a man and a writer is that he possesses the key to the past. His goal is to share these experiences and to unlock old treasures and rekindle old fires. He is the symbol of Yom Kippur, for he remembers.

True, this is his goal, but how does he envision the good life? How does he portray the good man? Is it one who sits and thinks only of the past? To articulate his point of view it is necessary to briefly relate another of his short stories, "Etzal Hemdat."

This short story relates the experiences of a young boy who, due to difficulties with his stepmother, is sent to the city and home of his father's old friend, Hemdat, a renowned cantor. Arriving in town on the day before Yom Kippur, he enters the synagogue to pray. There the gaiety and joy of the people are of such a spontaneous nature that he is urged to participate in their festivities and partake of their food and drink. Upon satiating himself, he asks the people to direct him to the home of Hemdat. While all appear to know the location of the cantor's home, few are able to present coherent directions to it. As a result, the lad begins to lose his way among the bewildering, unfamiliar mazes of the city. Finally, by chance, he happens upon the home of Hemdat. His first impression is one of disillusionment, for Hemdat does not at all appear like the eminent personality his father and the townspeople claim him to be. Not only are his features ordinary, but his voice does not seem to possess the quality expected of a great cantor. The boy's amazement does not end with his first meeting but continues to manifest itself.

Hemdat befriends the youth and takes him on a trip through town. All who meet the cantor are extremely cordial to him and freely offer him various delicacies which are warmly accepted. The cantor evinces not only a kind and cheerful disposition but also a great capacity for the absorption of food and drink.

A different aspect of the cantor's character is noted as the night of Yom Kippur daws near. Hemdat bathes himself and walks to the synagogue alone with his thoughts. The masses of people who have come to pray with him pave a path for their holy cantor. Hemdat walks to the podium and silently prepares himself for his prayers. His first sound is a heartbreaking moan of woe that forces the people to tremble and cry. As he begins to sing, his melodies are so sweet and meaningful, his voice so pure and full of emotion, that at times it appears as if a holy angel were standing on the podium beckoning the people to return and repent. Hemdat has the hearts of his people fused into his prayers. He is the true messenger of his people.

This brief narration is replete with philosophical and theological ramifications.

The Talmud states that he who eats and enjoys himself on the day before Yom Kippur is symbolically considered to have fasted on both this and the following day.[4] Here we find a unique contrast. Two days following each other; on the first, food and drink play an important role, on the second, the abstinence of these items marks its distinction. Materialism of one day is followed and ritualistically intertwined with the absolute spiritualism of the other.

On the day before Yom Kippur a young boy arrives in a town that knows how to enjoy the materialistic pleasures of the world. While he shares their gifts and partakes in their festivity, he does not become dissuaded from his task. He seeks Hemdat. He seeks the good man. The man everyone knows but cannot locate. After a tedious journey he meets the object of his search. He meets the man who is not marked by physical stature. A man who enjoys and, indeed, thrives on materialistic pleasures. Is this the good man?

On the night of Yom Kippur Hemdat manifests his true personality. He is one who does not allow the materialism of the world to withhold his religious fervor. He is one who is at home with the enjoyment of the world and the purity of religion. Neither sphere of influence is strange to him. He possesses and actually lives a complete life and thus is, indeed, the good man.

Many people are not able to combine these two approaches to life. One is usually emphasized to the detriment of the other. Agnon tells us to fuse the world of materialism and the world of spiritualism into a united whole. He reminds us to remember the twofold symbol of Yom Kippur and its preceding day. One tells us to eat and be merry, the other, to examine our past in preparation for the future.

We should view the world as the day before Yom Kippur. This implies that our orientation should not be of sadness but rather of joy and gaiety. At the same time we should not forget our moral and religious obligations. We should remember that the eve of Yom Kippur is followed by and interconnected with a day of piety and religious fervor. Our life should be guided by a fusion of the symbolic rituals of each day.

This is Agnon's message to mankind; this is his sermon to the Jew. This is the reason why he serves as the spiritual historian of our people. This is the reason his receipt of international acclaim brought glory to our religion itself. For Agnon was not a Hebrew writer but a writer of the soul of the Jew.

NOTES

1. *Tmol Shilshom* (Tel Aviv: Schocken, 1959), pp. 89–90.
2. *Bilav Yamin*, pp. 7, 38.
3. Ibid., p. 30.
4. *Yoma* 81b.

62. *The Shema*

The *Shema* is one of the most important prayers known to the Jew. It is of such significance that Jews recite it not only twice a day, but also in the last moment of their lives. This prayer poignantly portrays man's cardinal beliefs as well as the aim and goal which he strives to achieve. Much thought, much effort must be utilized in comprehending this deep, sacred commitment of faith. To enable one to gain but some insight into the vast implications of this most important prayer, the following brief study guide is presented. It will endeavor to translate and interpret the basic meanings of the first portion of the *Shema*. It should be noted that this guide is but a means to provoke thought and understanding of the daily prayers, and to make an inroad into the vast realm of our thought and action that the *Shema* certainly demands of all Jews.

Hear, O Israel, the Lord our God, the Lord is One.
Hear, O Israel: Shema Yisrael (Deut. 6:4-9).
    The word *shema* implies the physical aspect of hearing as well as the mental process of understanding. Jews are requested to listen and attempt to understand the meaningful patterns of Godliness.
Hear, O Israel
    When one recites the *Shema*, he must let himself hear what he says, for it is written "Hear, O Israel" (*Berachot* 15a).
Israel
    Yisrael (Israel), the name given to our patriarch Jacob, is also

204

the all-inclusive term by which the entire congregation of Jewry is known. The word *Yisrael*, which means *yahsher eem Hashem*, "upright and wholehearted with God," poignantly defines the essential characteristic and raison d'être of all Jews. We are a religious community whose cardinal aim and primary goal is to serve God and follow His commandments. No other aim, no other project is valid. Our life, our morality must be intertwined with our religious and divine commitments.

Yisrael also means reign, rule, and nobility. The Jewish religion is a sacred, lofty, and noble endeavor. No one should be ashamed of its concepts. Each Jew should be proud and happy to follow the Torah and walk in the path of its holy doctrines.

Hear, O Israel

You, who are members of the *noble, religious community* called Israel should certainly *hear* and attempt to *understand* all that is holy, and all that is good.

Hear, O Israel

This is also a proclamation of the high sacred status of Israel. It is a statement defining Israel's special relationship to God. Israel listens and understands spiritual values. Individual Jews may falter and neglect to obey the laws of the Torah, but Israel, the entire Jewish community, the Jewish nation as a whole, has traditionally always hearkened to the word of God. The Jewish nation received the Torah from Mount Sinai and historically cherished its laws throughout periods of prosperity or danger. Israel hears, Israel knows that its future depends on its constant listening and following of the commandments of the Torah.

The Lord is our God

God, the creator, ruler, and lawgiver of the universe, identifies himself with the Jewish nation. *He is our God*. He has presented us with a Torah and guides as well as oversees all our thoughts, actions, and deeds.

The Lord is our God

The *Shem Havayah*, the four-lettered word signifying God, which begin with the letters aleph, daled, portrays the sublime characteristics of our God. It means that He is outside the limitations of time. To Him the past, present, and future are all one.

His name is pronounced in Hebrew in the same fashion as one would say "my master, my lord." This is the recognition each Jew must have that God is in reality the master of man's destiny. His divine will and providence guide and influence our daily lives.

The Lord is our God

The phrase *Hashem Elokaynu* is found in many diverse places throughout our prayers. In fact, no *berachah*, no blessing, is proper without its inclusion. The Gaon of Vilna, Rabbi Elijah, once said that while the word *Hashem* refers to the essence of God, to that which is most difficult to apprehend and comprehend in all its ramifications, the term *Elokaynu* suggests those aspects of God that are revealed to man—His Torah, His miracles, His works, and divine providence and presence. A firm believer is one who firmly combines both elements into one unifying whole. Our God, because He is God and above human reason, is difficult to completely define, yet we see and observe His manifestations in so many ways, by His Torah, by His guidance, by the structured plan of the world, and by His direct control of all events.

The Lord is our God

Hashem Elokaynu also refers to the dual role of God. He is revealed to man as *Hashem*, the God of love, mercy, and compassion. At the same time He is *Elokaynu*, the ideal personification of law and justice. God is the unique and miraculous synthesis of mercy and justice, law and compassion.

The Lord is one

Just as God is one, so too is Israel. To flourish, Israel must in some way strive to imitate the unity of God by displaying brotherhood and mutual responsibility for the deeds of all their brethren.

The Lord is one

The Talmud relates that just as God is one, so too will a period of time come about wherein the oneness and unity of love and happiness will be present in the lives of all. There will be a time wherein there will be no distinction between good and bad, happiness and misfortune, gaiety and sorrow. All will be good, all will be happy.

Hear, O Israel, the Lord our God, the Lord is one

The *Shema* is the concrete vehicle by which twice a day, Jews observe the first two commandments of the ten commandments heard on Sinai.

Blessed be His name, whose glorious kingdom is forever and ever

Does God need man's blessing? No. Some, therefore, interpret the word *baruch* to mean "the fountain of all blessings." This prayer would then mean, "God's holy name is the fountain of all blessings, and His kingdom is forever and ever."

Jews are proud to assert, accept, and proclaim to all that God is the Father of mankind and His rule is forever.

And thou shall love thy God with all thy heart, and with all thy soul and with all thy might

And thou shall love thy God

How can the Torah command man to love God? Is not love a quality that you either have or do not have? Is it not a feeling that can only be expressed spontaneously, without force or compulsion? Jews believe that within each man there is an innate capacity and reservoir of love for God. This love is inactive and must be worked upon to bring it into its full potentiality. The Torah does not want this love to be idle or decayed through disuse. Jews are required to develop their potentialities and bring into a concrete reality the beautiful love of man for God.

An element of love is a feeling of identification and binding unity. These emotions should also be experienced in man's intimate relationship with God.

And thou shall love thy God with all thy heart

The Talmud related that the Hebrew term *levavcha* is plural and thus connotes that both man's good inclinations (*yetzer tov*) and bad inclinations (*yetzer horah*) should be utilized for the service of God. To serve with one's good inclinations means that such attributes as mercy, love, kindness, graciousness, and loyalty should be directed toward the enhancement of religious values.

To serve God with one's bad inclinations means that such qualities as hatred, anger, animosity, and hostility should be used in a positive fashion by being directed at that which is corrupt and evil.

And thou shall love thy God . . . with all thy soul

The Talmud maintains that one should sacrifice life itself rather than forsake one's belief in God. This is the pinnacle of love, for in this act man poignantly manifests that his love of God is more important than even his own personal well-being.

And thou shall love thy God . . . with all thy might

Power and strength are not alien to religion. One should not believe that religion is only for the meek. One who has power, one who has the means of influencing people, should not shy away from becoming a forceful vehicle in combating all that is wrong and all that needs to be eliminated. It also means that one should not be basically a Jew only in one's heart. Time, effort, energy, and money should be devoted to the cause of enhancing religiosity and Judaism.

And with all thy might

The biblical term *m'odecha* is interpreted to mean your *medot*, your attributes. This means that every attribute by which a man is noted should be channeled toward the sphere of religion. Each person is a unique and distinct personality. Each has qualities that are not found in another. These unique qualities should be used toward making a personal distinct contribution to Judaism.

And with all thy might

M'odecha is also defined as "your wealth." Affluence must be utilized for religious values. Money can purchase mitzvot and serve Godliness.

And these words which I command thee this day shall be upon thy heart

Each day one should feel as if the Torah were once again presented to man. Each day the Torah should be conceived as something new and invigorating. Each day one should learn something new, something different.

And thou shall teach them diligently to thy children and shall talk of them when thou sittest in thy house, when thou walkest by the way, and when thou liest down, and when thou risest up.

And thou shall teach them diligently to thy children

One who honestly believes in a doctrine will teach it diligently to his children. One who acts merely through habit or force will not endeavor to transmit such a rule to his children.

And thou shall teach them . . . to thy children and shall talk of them

Your manner of teaching shall be in the same fashion as your usual mode of talking with your children. Parents who are able to talk and discuss things with their children are able to teach them.

. . . and shall talk of them

The formulation of proper thoughts is expressed by words. By speaking, relating, and recounting the idea of God, His wisdom, power, and goodness one is stimulated and motivated to a better belief and a more meaningful way of life. On the converse, by relating continually that which is corrupt or evil one tends to think along those lines. So, man must be trained to guard his speech.

When thou sittest in thy house, when thou walkest by the way, when thou liest down and when thou risest up

The study of Torah and the observance of its commandments cannot be limited to but one segment of a Jew's life. All activities, all periods of time must be utilized for the proper development of one's religious goals.

. . . when thou liest down and when thou risest up

Our sages in the Talmud derive from these words that one is required to say the 'Shema' in the morning and evening of each day. The Biblical phrase does not mean that at the exact moment of awakening in the morning or retiring in the evening one must say the *Shema*. The Biblical phrase rather refers to the period when people generally awake and the period when people generally sleep.

And thou shall Bind them for a sign upon thine hand, and they shall be for frontlets between thy eyes. And thou shall write them upon the door-posts of thy house, and upon thy gates.

Man tends to forget. He must continuously be reminded of his moral and spiritual obligations. He must never be allowed to stray from the path of the Torah, the way of guidance and correct behavior. For this reason he is commanded to daily recall his committment to Judaism by wearing 'Teffilin'. The 'Teffilin' are worn near the brain and near the heart to show that both are used for the service of God.

The Jew's home and every room within it must bear the mark of a "mezzuzah" which is to remind him that a home is a sanctuary for religioius and ethical patterns.

On each Mezzuzah, three Hebrew letters may be noted: Shin, Dalad, Yud. They represent: 1. The name of Almighty God; to signify the *mark* of God on each Jewish home. 2. An abbreviation of the Hebrew phrase "Shomayr D'Latot Yisrael"—Guardian of Jewish Doors. The home is guarded by the presence of God. It's safe to enter. It's secure for residence.

63. *Pidyon Habayn*
The Redemption of the Firstborn Son

The redemption of the firstborn son is a ritual ceremony of biblical origin. Scripture states:

> And every firstborn of man, among thy children shalt thou redeem. And it shall be when thy son asketh thee in time to come, saying: What is this? That thou shalt say unto him: By strength of hand did God bring us out from Egypt, out of the house of bondage; and it came to pass when Pharaoh was stubborn not to let us go, that God slew all the firstborn in the land of Egypt, from the firstborn of man to the firstborn of beast; therefore . . . every firstborn of my sons do I redeem (Exodus 13:13–15).

The ceremony, therefore, is an ever-reoccurring reminder that ancient Jewish freedom from bondage occurred through the traumatic destruction of the Egyptian firstborn. The Jewish children were the only firstborn which miraculously survived the tenth plague. Thus, each firstborn son became a symbol of Jewish survival and divine providence and was at first to be dedicated to a priestly, God-serving vocation. The mandate of redemption is a lesson to all that spiritual and moral life need not be separated from the family. The aim of Jewish life is not to prepare holy men for service in a temple. For, indeed, it is the Jewish home which is the altar for religious survival. The firstborn were to be like all other children, yet a model for Jewish living. The ritual redemption from the *kohan* (priest) is the commitment of each parent to the principle that religious leadership has a mission within the ordinary life of family experiences.

The ceremony is conducted by placing the child in the hands of the *kohan*, who requests of the parents, "Which do you prefer—your firstborn son or five silver dollars?"

Historically, the *kohanim* (priests) were the masters of Jewish law and the teachers of knowledge.

The question is an attempt to ascertain the parental commitment to the education of his child. The *kohan*, the educator and teacher, wishes to know whether the parent will commit himself to expend funds to teach his child Torah and knowledge. Any parent who values money more than the intellectual and moral growth of his child does not deserve to have a Jewish child. By giving the money to the *kohan*, each father is symbolically announcing his firm commitment to sacrifice for the stature of his son.

The five silver dollars represent the amount the brothers of Joseph received for selling him into slavery. The father wishes it known that no child of his will ever seek gain at the expense of another family member. Just the opposite. Money is a vehicle to acquire knowledge, morality, and good deeds. It is given to the *kohan* to serve the cause of all.

64. Jewish Time

The Jew is unique; so too is his calculation of time. A calendar change occurs not at midnight or at sunrise, but, rather, with sunset and the onset of the darkness of the night. Accordingly, all Jewish observances of Shabbat and festivals commence at sundown. Birthdates, anniversaries, historical events all follow this procedure.

Some maintain that this custom is derived from the biblical description of creation, wherein, at the conclusion of each day, it states, "and there was evening and there was morning" (Genesis 1). Thus, the day follows the evening preceding it.

Yet it has been suggested that this verse is but a description of chronological events rather than a mandate for calculating a day change. The rationale is that Scripture itself implies a day calculation contrary to the above formulation; namely, that the night follows the day. Upon conclusion of the deluge, God vows never again to curse the earth because of man's sake. He says, "While the earth remains, seed time and harvest, and cold and heat, summer and winter, and *day and night* shall not cease" (Genesis 8:22), R. Pinchas HaLevi Horowitz (1730–1805, Frankfurt, author of *Panim Yafot*) notes that the phrase "and day and night shall not cease" lends credence to the view that a full calendar day was the combination of the day and the night subsequent to it.

Jewish time, as it is practiced today, is, rather, derived from the verse "From evening to evening shall you celebrate your Sabbath" (Leviticus 23:32). This phrase deals with the observ-

213

ance of Yom Kippur. It is a specific imperative detailing the actual time parameters of the holiday. Accordingly, the day follows the night preceding it. To the extent that this law is an integral part of the statutes given to Moses on Mount Sinai. Jewish time is, therefore, an innovation that occurred at Sinai. Hence, contends the *Panim Yafot*, prior to Sinai and the revelation, a day change was reckoned differently. Namely, during the era of the Patriarchs and the Egyptian bondage, a day was considered the morning and the evening following it. A calendar date change took place at sunrise.

R. Moshe Sofer (Pressberg, 1762–1839), author of the *Hatam Sofer* (see *Derashot Shavuot)*, utilized this theory of his rebbe (R. Horowitz) to explain why Shavuot is celebrated as a two-day holiday. The Bible does not fix the date of the month for the Shavuot holiday; it merely states, "And you shall count for yourselves from the morrow after the Sabbath. . . . seven complete Sabbaths shall there be: To the morrow after the seventh Sabbath shall you number fifty days" (Leviticis 23:15–16). The Talmud rules that the phrase "the morrow after the Sabbath" means the day after the first day of Passover, not Shabbat (*Menachot* 65b). If so, then Shavuot should always come out on the fiftieth day of the counting of the omer. The second day of Shavuot is the fifty-first day of the omer. As such, it has no relationship to the biblical mandate. For the holiday as it is noted in the Bible relates to the omer, not the revelation.

The *Hatam Sofer* provides the following rationale. Prior to the revelation, each day began at sunrise and concluded at the following sunrise. The Jews began to count the omer on the second day of Passover at sunrise. Tradition has it that the revelation at Mount Sinai transpired in the morning prior to sunrise at the coming of the dawn *(Amud HaShachar)*. Hence, it was the fiftieth day of the omer. To the extent, however, that revelation crystallized a new concept of time, namely, that a date change occurs at the evening preceding the day, such a period was the fifty-first day according to the new method of calculating time.

Accordingly, both days are presently celebrated (in the diaspora) to symbolically record the date-change transformation that took place on Mount Sinai.

Days of the Week

Jewish custom does not designate each day of the week with a specific name. Such common names as Sunday, Monday, Tuesday, Wednesday, Thursday, and Friday are alien to Jewish tradition. Instead, each day is described in relationship to Shabbat, the seventh day of the week. Accordingly, Sunday is called the first day of the Shabbat, Monday the second day of the Shabbat, . . . Friday the sixth day of the Shabbat. This procedure is a means of observing the mitzvah of Zachor—"Remember the Sabbath to keep it holy" (Exodus 20:8). Shabbat is, therefore, remembered not only on the seventh day but throughout each day of the week (see Ramban). At the conclusion of the daily morning prayers (Shacharit) the Jew recites a phrase detailing the day of the week. This affords him with a daily biblical mitzvah of remembering Shabbat directly prior to his regular activities. It is also a vehicle to ensure that Shabbat will be remembered at its proper time.

Weeks

A week is seven days and concludes with Shabbat, the holy day of rest. This segment of time has no scientific geophysical basis. (Days relate to the rotation of the earth upon its axis, months to lunar activity, and years to the earth's movement around the solar system.) A seven-day week is solely derived from the biblical description of creation. As such, international movements to increase the number of days in the week have firmly been decried by Jewish leaders as dangerous precedents which undermine Sabbath observance.

HaGaon Rav Hutner (z.l.) once noted that the term "weekend" is generally misused even by observant Jews. Custom (specifically advertisements) refers to both Saturday and Sunday as a weekend. This is not the Jewish way. To the Jew the weekend concludes on Saturday night. Once Shabbat is over it is no longer the "weekend."

Months

Jewish months have specific names (Nisan, Iyar, Sivan, Tamuz, Av, Elul, Tishrei, Heshvon, Kislev, Taivet, Shevat, Adar). Yet such names are not located in Scripture. Biblical months relate to the Exodus. The first month (Nisan) is described in the Bible as merely the first month, coinciding with the Exodus from Egypt. Holidays are also detailed as occurring in a day of a month relating to the Exodus. For example, Rosh Hashanah and Yom Kippur are not noted to transpire in Tishrei. The Bible states that Rosh Hashanah takes place on the first day of the seventh month. Starting with the Exodus (Nisan), this means that the above-noted holidays occur during the month of Tishrei (the seventh month). (See Leviticus 23:24, 27.)

The Ramban suggests that the common Hebrew names for the months were instituted during the Babylonian exile. Just as the Exodus served as the pivotal frame of reference for the counting of the months, so too was the subsequent redemption such a standard. In other words, months relate to redemption from exile. The sages instituted proper names for the months to perpetually record the subsequent exile.

The months are sanctified at religious services on the Shabbat preceding the coming of a new moon. It includes a special ritual prayer linking Rosh Chodesh to redemption from slavery. As such, the new month is a symbol of potential freedom. The lunar calendar teaches the Jew never to despair. The moon may be dark, it may not be full. So, too, is life. All blessings may not be noted. But the moon will shine again. In time it will be seen. So too will the joy of freedom and prosperity.

The Year

The Jewish year commences with Rosh Hashanah (the first day of the seventh month dating from the Exodus). Years relate to commitment and judgment. This means that progress, joy, and success are not automatically guaranteed for the coming year. They must be deserved. Man must recognize that life itself is a trial.

Jewish time is therefore unique. It is a means of relating segments of life to religious principles and values. It is a constant reminder of the ideological beliefs of the Jew.